Real Estate Math
Thoroughly Explained

All the Math that Every Salesperson
and Broker Needs to Know

by

Jim Bainbridge, J.D.

© 2015

City Breeze Publishing
P.O. Box 12650
Marina del Rey, California 90295

ISBN: 978-1-939526-27-4

PRINTED IN THE UNITED STATES OF AMERICA

About the Author

Jim Bainbridge is a graduate of Harvard Law School and has been an active member of the California Bar for more than 30 years. He is a licensed California real estate broker, and a past recipient of a National Science Foundation Fellowship for graduate studies in mathematics at UC Berkeley, where as a TA he taught numerous mathematics courses to university students.

Mr. Bainbridge is the author of 14 books, including *California Real Estate Principles and License Preparation*. Additionally, his work has been published in more than 50 journals in the USA, UK, Canada, Australia, Japan, and the Netherlands. He is also a member of the Real Estate Educators Association (REEA), and has been recognized as a Certified Distance Education Instructor by IDECC, which is a function of the Association of Real Estate License Law Officials.

DISCLAIMER and LIMIT of LIABILITY

Preface

Because nearly all real estate transactions involve numbers, and because approximately 5% to 10% of the problems on most real estate license exams involve numerical calculations, real estate professionals — and aspiring real estate professionals — should become reasonably proficient in solving the most frequently encountered real-estate-related math problems. Fortunately for those who are not particularly fond of working with mathematics, only the very basic concepts of arithmetic, algebra, and geometry are required to easily handle the math aspects of problems on real estate license exams, as well as most of the math issues encountered by real estate salespersons, brokers, and investors.

This book is designed to familiarize real estate students and professionals with all of the basic math concepts that apply to day-to-day real estate transaction issues. The reader who works through this book will become familiar with — and hopefully proficient in — the math necessary to easily solve math problems on real estate license exams, and to be aware of the important math implications of decisions made by sellers, buyers, and agents in real estate transactions.

Table of Contents

CHAPTER 1: LENGTH, AREA, AND VOLUME

Units of Measure.

Length:

1 foot (1ft. or 1') = 12 inches (12 in. or 12")
1 yard (yd.) = 3 feet = 36 inches
1 rod = 5.5 yd. = 16.5 ft.
1 mile = 320 rods = 1,760 yd. = 5,280 ft.

Area:

1 sq. ft. = 12 in. × 12 in. = 144 sq. in. (144 in.²)
1 sq. yd. = 3 ft. × 3 ft. = 9 sq. ft. (9 ft.²)
1 acre = 43,560 sq. ft. = 4,840 sq. yd. (4,840 yd.²) = 160 sq. rods
1 section = 1 sq. mile = 640 acres = 1/36 township

30.25 sq. rod

Volume (Cubic):

1 cu. ft. = 12 in. × 12 in. × 12 in. = 1,728 cu. in.³
1 cu. yd. = 3 ft. × 3 ft. × 3 ft. = 27 cu. ft.

Area Calculations.

When calculating the area of something (usually expressed in square feet), remember that the area of a rectangle is base × height and the area of a triangle is ½ (base × height) or (base × height) ÷ 2.

Example: A 12 ft. by 20 ft. rectangular living room is going to be carpeted with wall-to-wall carpeting, having an installed price of six dollars per square foot. What is the total cost of this carpeting job?

height: 12 ft.   Area = base × height

base: 20 ft.

Answer: The area of this living room is 20 ft. × 12 ft. = 240 sq. ft. Therefore, the cost of the carpet is 240 ft.² × $6/ft.² = $1,440.

Example: A lot of land in the shape of a right triangle with height 80' ft. and base 170'sells for $35 per square foot. What is the cost of this lot?

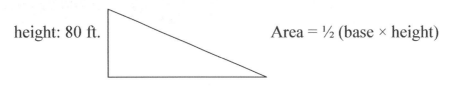

height: 80 ft.   Area = ½ (base × height)

base: 170 ft.

Answer: The area of this lot is ½ (80 ft. × 170 ft.) = 6,800 ft.² Therefore, the cost of the lot is 6,800 ft.² × $35/ft.² = $238,000.

Example: What is the area of the triangle in the diagram below?

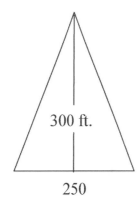

300 ft.

250

Answer: The area of this triangle, as with all triangles, is equal to ½ (base × height), which in this case is ½ (250 ft. × 300 ft.) = 37,500 sq. ft.

Example: What is the area of the office building in the following diagram?

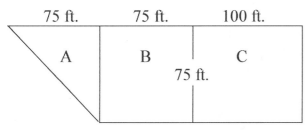

75 ft.   75 ft.   100 ft.

A   B   C

75 ft.

Answer: Section A is a triangle having a base of 75 ft. and the height of 75 ft., so the area of section A is ½ (75 ft. × 75 ft.) = 2,812.5 ft.²

Section B is a square, in which the base = height. Therefore, the area of section B is 75 ft. × 75 ft. = 5,625 ft.²

Section C is a rectangle, in which the base = 100 ft. and the height = 75 ft. Therefore, the area of section C is 100 ft. × 75 ft. = 7,500 ft.², giving a total area of 2,812.5 ft.² + 5,625 ft.² + 7,500 ft.² = 15,937.5 ft.²

Example: Kevin is going to purchase the lot shown in the figure below and build on it a house and garage, also shown in the figure below. He has been quoted the following: $150 per square foot for the house; $40 per square foot for the garage; $10 per square foot for the land. What is the total amount that Kevin will pay for this lot, house, and garage?

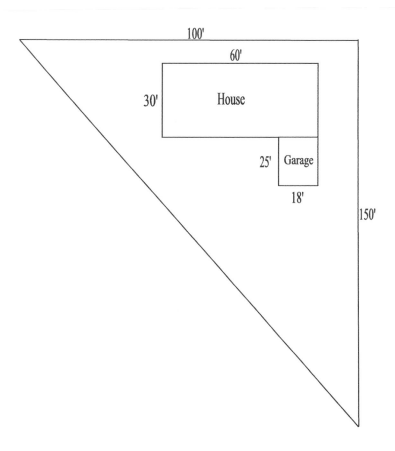

Answer: First we calculate the square footage of each item:

house area = 60' × 30' = 1,800 ft.²

garage area = 25' × 18' = 450 ft.²

lot area = ½ (100' × 150') = 7,500 ft.²

cost of house = 1,800 ft.² × $150 per ft.² = $270,000

cost of garage = 450 ft.² × $40 per ft.² = $18,000

cost of the lot = 7,500 ft.² × $10 per ft.² = $75,000

Total = $363,000

In the real world, not all land lots and floor spaces are perfect squares, rectangles, or triangles. Correspondingly, not all area-related problems on real estate exams concern perfect squares, rectangles or triangles.

Example: A residential lot on a hillside has a northern border of 120 feet, a western border of 60 feet, and a southern border of 100 feet. The northern and southern borders are parallel to each other and the angle between each and the western border is 90°. What is the area of this lot?

Answer: If a diagram is not included in the question, it would be helpful as a first step to sketch a diagram of the lot so that you have a visual rendition of the word problem.

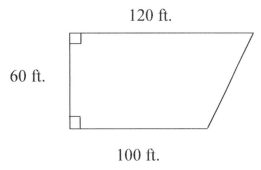

When presented with a non-regular lot or floor space, try to deconstruct the area into rectangles and triangles, the areas of which you know how to easily calculate. Looking at the above diagram, you should be able to imagine this residential lot as consisting of one rectangle and one triangle, as shown in the diagram below.

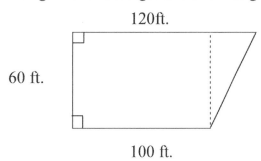

Now we have an area we can calculate: one rectangle that has a base of 100 ft. and a height of 60 ft., and one triangle with a base of 20 ft. and a height of 60 ft. Therefore, the area of this lot is (60' × 100') + ½ (20' × 60') = 6,000 ft.² + 600 ft.² = 6,600 ft.²

Rectangular Survey System

Calculations of area in regard to the rectangular survey system of legal land descriptions frequently appear on real estate license exams. The rectangular survey system (also referred to as the U.S. government survey system) is based on first establishing principal east-west base line(s) and north-south meridian(s). Extending these principal base line(s) and meridian(s), a grid of horizontal lines, referred to as tier lines, running parallel to the principal base line(s), and vertical lines, referred to as range lines, is established. The tier lines are 6 miles apart, as are the range lines.

A section is an area one square mile, containing 640 acres. Creating sections of 640 acres makes for ease of dividing into halves, quarters, and so on through seven divisions, down to 5 acres. A township is a six mile square parcel of land consisting of 36 sections. The sections in each township are uniformly numbered from 1 to 36, with Section 1 located in the northeast corner and the Section 36 located in the southeast corner.

A theoretical township showing numbered sections							
(large bold type) and adjacent township sections (smaller regular type).							
36	31	32	33	34	35	36	31
1	**6**	**5**	**4**	**3**	**2**	**1**	6
12	**7**	**8**	**9**	**10**	**11**	**12**	7
13	**18**	**17**	**16**	**15**	**14**	**13**	18
24	**19**	**20**	**21**	**22**	**23**	**24**	19
25	**30**	**29**	**28**	**27**	**26**	**25**	30
36	**31**	**32**	**33**	**34**	**35**	**36**	31
1	6	5	4	3	2	1	6

← RANGE LINES →

← TIER LINES →

For example, the description "township 3 north, range 2 east, Stonyfield Base Line and Meridian" (typically abbreviated as "T3N, R2E, SBL&M") is a description of the township that is 3 townships north from the Stonyfield Base Line and 2 townships east from the Stonyfield Meridian.

When working with legal land descriptions based on the rectangular survey system, it is helpful to remember the following:

o   1 acre = 43,560 square feet

o   1 square acre ≈ 208.7 ft. × 208.7 ft.

o   1 mile = 5,280 feet or 320 rods

o   1 rod = 16½ ft.

- o 1 township = 6 mile × 6 mile = 36 sections
- o 1 section = 1 mile × 1 mile = 640 acres

Because a section contains 640 acres, a quarter section contains 160 acres. Parts of a section are often described using direction abbreviations and fractions. For example, the 160-acre northwest quarter of Section 15 would be described as "the NW¼ of Section 15."

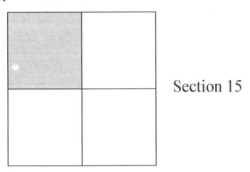

Section 15

The 40-acre southeast quarter of the southeast quarter of Section 15 would be described as "the SE¼ of the SE¼ of Section 11."

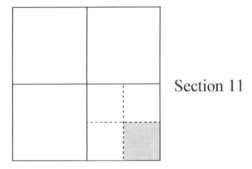

Section 11

Example: What is the rectangular survey system legal description of the shaded area of Section 10 in the diagram below?

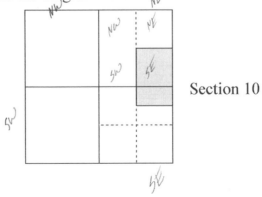

Section 10

Answer: Because the shaded area extends into two distinct quarters of the section, we need to analyze each of the separate shaded areas separately. The smaller area is in the SE¼ of the section, is in the NE¼ of the SE¼ of Section 10, and is in the N½ of the NE¼ of the SE¼ of Section 10. The larger area is in the NE¼ of Section 10, and is in the SE¼ of the NE¼ quarter of Section 10.

Example: How many acres are in the SW¼ of the NW¼ of the SW¼ of Section 3?

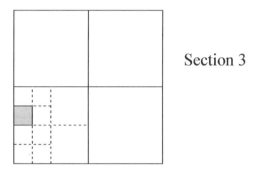

Section 3

Answer: Because there are 640 acres in every section, the SW¼ of Section 3 contains 640 acres ÷ 4 = 160 acres. Similarly, the NW¼ of the SW¼ contains 160 acres ÷ 4 = 40 acres, and the SW¼ of the NW¼ of the SW¼ contains 40 acres ÷ 4 = 10 acres.

Example: Which of the following parcels of Section 5 in the following diagram is described as the NW¼ of the SE¼ of Section 5?

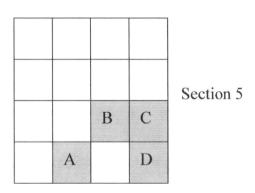

Section 5

Answer: First, locate the SE¼ of Section 5, which is the quarter section containing parcels B, C, and D. Next, it is apparent that parcel B is the NW¼ of that SE¼ of Section 5.

Example: How many acres are there in 204,732 ft.²?

a. 4.81 acres

b. 4.78 acres

c. 4.57 acres

d. none of the above

Answer: **d**. 204,732 ft.² ÷ 43,560 ft.²/acre = 4.7 acres.

Length Calculations.

Because the area of a rectangle equals the length of the base times the length of the height, if we know the area of a rectangle and the length of its base, we can calculate the length its height.

Example: The area of a rectangle is 4,572 ft.², and its base is 36 ft. What is the height of this rectangle?

Answer: We know that 36 ft. × (the height) = 4,572 ft.². Therefore, the height = 4,572 ft.² ÷ 36 ft. = 127 ft.

Example: A square lot of 200 feet on each side has a building setback of 25 feet from each side. What is the maximum square footage of a three-story office building that can be built on this lot?

Answer: This problem requires us to solve two issues: the first concerns what is the maximum footprint of a building due to a setback regulation; the second concerns the fact that the question informed us that the building would have three stories. First, because of the 25 ft. setback on each side, the maximum footprint of the building would be 150 ft. × 150 ft. = 22,500 ft.².   Second, because the building has three stories, the maximum square footage of the building would be 22,500 ft.² × 3 = 67,500 ft.².

Example: Jennifer owns a rectangular lot that is 175 feet deep and 105 feet wide. She has contracted to have a 4½ foot high fence built around the lot. Materials cost will be $.55 per square foot and the labor cost will be $2.15 per linear foot. What will the fence cost Jennifer?

Answer: This problem requires us to solve three issues: the first concerns how many linear feet of fence it will take to enclose this rectangular lot; the second concerns how many square feet of fencing there will be and what will be the cost at $.55 per *square* foot ; the third concerns the labor cost calculated at $2.15 per *linear* foot. *First*, the rectangular lot has four sides — two sides at 175 feet and two sides at 105 feet, totaling 560 linear feet. *Second*, because the fence is 4½ ft. high and runs for 560 ft., the fence consists of 4½ ft. × 560 ft. = 2,520 ft.² At a materials cost of $.55 per square foot, the cost of the fencing materials is 2,520 ft.² × $.55/ ft.² = $1,386. *Third*, because the fence runs for 560 linear feet, and the labor cost is $2.15 per linear foot, the labor cost for the fence is 560 ft. × $2.15/ft. = $1,204. Adding the fencing cost and labor cost together, we get $1,386 + $1,204 = $2,590.

Example: A triangular lot with a height 105 feet and a base of 95 feet sold for $12 per square foot. What did the lot sell for?

Answer: The area of the triangular lot is ½ (105 ft. × 95 ft.) = 4,987.5 ft.². Therefore, at a cost of $12/ ft.², the lot sold for 4,987.5 ft.² × $12/ft.² = $59,850.

Example: A road runs along the west side of a section. If the road is 45 feet wide how many acres does the part of the road just to the west of the S½ of the NW¼ of the section contain?

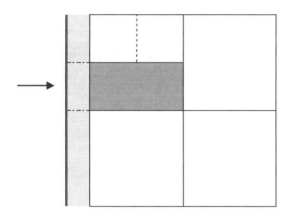

Answer: As with nearly all questions containing a rectangular survey system legal description, it is best to start out by drawing a diagram described in the word problem. Because each side of a section is 1 mile = 5,280 ft. in length, the part of the road just to the west of the S½ of the NW¼ of the section is 5,280 ft ÷ 4 = 1,320 ft. long. As seen in the diagram, the "part of the road" we are looking for is a rectangle, 1,320 ft. long and 45 ft. wide. Therefore, this part of the road is 1,320 ft. × 45 ft. = 59,400 ft.².
59,400 ft.² ÷ 43,560 ft.²/acre = 1.364 acres (rounded).

Volume Calculations.

Real estate agents who deal with commercial property — especially warehouse or industrial properties — need to be familiar with volume calculations. Warehouse and industrial properties typically are in the form of rectangular boxes, for which volume is calculated as length × width × height.

Example: A warehouse is 15 yards wide, 25 yards long, and 28 feet high. How many cubic feet are contained in this warehouse?

Answer: The first thing we must do to perform calculations on problems that contain mixed units of measure — as does this example — is to convert all measurements to the same dimension. Because the question asks for how many cubic feet, it makes most sense to convert yards into feet, rather than feet into yards. Doing this, the volume of this warehouse is

(15 yd. × 3 ft./yd.) × (25 yd. × 3 ft./yd.) × 28 ft. = 94,500 cu. ft.

Example: You have a client who needs to lease or purchase a warehouse with a capacity of 34,020 cubic feet. Your client tells you that for the goods that she intends to warehouse, the capacity of a warehouse is calculated according to the following formula: Capacity = 70% of (length × width × (height -1 yard)). You have located a rectangular warehouse having a length of 60 ft. and a width of 30 ft. What does the minimum height of this warehouse need to be to satisfy your client's needs?

Answer: To answer this problem, we translate the word problem written in English into the language of algebra, as we learned to do in first-year algebra class:

34,020 ft.^{3} = .7 (60 ft. × 30 ft. × (H - 3 ft.)), where H represents the minimum height in feet of the building. Dividing both sides of the equation by .7, we get

48,600 ft.^{3} = 60 ft. × 30 ft. × (H - 3 ft.).

48,600 ft.^{3} = 1,800 ft.^{2} H − 5,400 ft.^{3}

54,000 ft.^{3} = 1,800 ft.^{2} H

30 ft. = H

Chapter 1 Quiz

Question 1: Andrew wants to build a swimming pool 12' × 54' × 9'. How many cubic yards of earth must be excavated to provide the necessary space for this pool?

a. 5,832

b. 216

c. 648

d. 1,944

Question 2: The area of a triangle is 90 ft.², and its base is 12 ft. What is the height of this triangle?

a. 7.5 ft.

b. 12 ft.

c. 3.75 ft.

d. 15 ft.

Question 3: How many square yards are there in 54 acres?

a. 2,352,240

b. 261,360

c. 784,080

d. 87,120

Question 4: Colin owns a rectangular 3 acre lot, which he intends to divide into 12 equal lots each having a width of 120 ft. What would be the depth of each lot?

a. 272.25 ft.

b. 90.75 ft.

c. 1,089 ft.

d. 363 ft.

Question 5: Four contiguous rectangular lots each have a depth of 30 yards and a width of 40⅓ yards. What is the total acreage of these lots?

a. .11 acres (rounded)

b. .25 acres

c. .22 acres (rounded)

d. 1 acre

Question 6: A property described as the W½ of the NW¼ and the SW¼ of the SE ¼ of the E½ of Section 2 contains how many acres?

a.100

b.80

c.120

d. none of the above

Question 7: How many square feet are there in 3.5 acres?

a. 130,680 ft.²

b.152,460 ft.²

c. 148,960 ft.²

d. 127,680 ft.²

Question 8: Ernesto owns a 300 yd.² rectangular lot with frontage of 50 feet. What is the depth of Ernesto's lot?

a. 6 yards

b. 54 feet

c. 9 yards

d. 18 feet

Question 9: Susan owns a 2-acre rectangular lot and wishes to divide it into 4 lots of equal size, each having a depth of 200 feet. What would be the width of each of these lots?

a. 108.9 feet

b. 217.8 feet

c. 217.8 feet

d. 217.8 feet

Question 10: Bryan wants to build a storage shed in his backyard that will have a volume of 50 yd.³. After examining available space, he sees that he can build a shed 25 feet wide and 6 feet deep. What is the minimum height that Brian must build his storage shed in order to accommodate his desired 50 yd.³ of storage volume?

a. 3 ft.

b. 9 ft.

c. 6 ft.

d. none of the above.

Question 11: How many acres are there in 58,080 yd.²

a. 12 acres

b. 1⅓ acres

c. 4 acres

d. 8 acres

Question 12: What is the area of the office building in the following diagram?

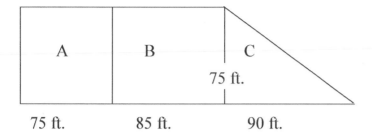

75 ft.   85 ft.   90 ft.

a. 14,625 ft.²

b. 18,750 ft.²

c. 15,375 ft.²

d. 12,562.5 ft.²

Question 13: Amanda purchased two vacant lots, A and B, for $124,000. Lot B cost $17,000 less than lot A. What did Amanda pay for lot B?

a. $53,500

b. $62,000

c. $70,500

d. none of the above

Question 14: What is the area of the lot in the following diagram, wherein all angles are right angles except for the angles created by the diagonal line?

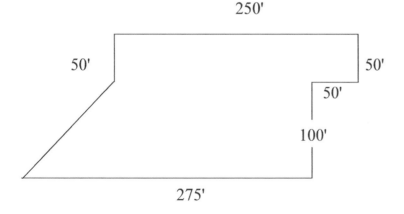

a. 25,250 ft.²

b. 35,000 ft.²

c. 36,250 ft.²

d. none of the above

Question 15: What is the rectangular survey system legal description of the shaded area of Section 8 in the diagram below?

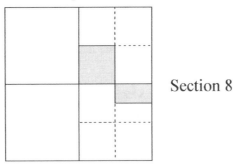 Section 8

a. SE¼ of the NE½ Section 8 and the NW¼ of the SE¼ of the SE¼ of Section 8

b. N½ of the NE¼ of the SE¼ of Section 8 and the N½ of the SW¼ of Section 8

c. N½ of the NE¼ of the SE¼ of Section 8 and the SE¼ of the NE¼ of Section 8

d. SW¼ of the NE¼ of Section 8 and the N½ of the NE¼ of the SE¼ of Section 8

Chapter 1 Quiz Answers

1.   **b.** $12' \times 54' \times 9' = 5{,}832$ ft.^{3}. There are 27 ft.^{3} in 1 yd.^{3}, therefore $5{,}832$ ft.$^3 \div 27$ ft.^{3}/yd.$^3 = 216$ yd.^{3}.

2.   **d.** The area of a triangle $= \frac{1}{2}$ (base $\times$ height). Therefore, in this case, 90 ft.$^2 = \frac{1}{2}$ (12 ft. $\times$ height). Multiplying both sides of the equation by two, 180 ft.$^2 = 12$ ft. $\times$ height. Dividing both sides of the equation by 12, 15 ft. $=$ height.

3.   **b.** There are 43,560 ft.^{2}/acre, so in 54 acres there are there are 43,560 ft.$^2 \times 54 = 2{,}352{,}240$ ft.^{2} in 54 acres. There are 9 ft.^{2}/yd.^{2}, so 2,352,240 ft.$^2 \div 9$ ft.^{2}/yd.$^2 = 261{,}360$ yd.^{2} in 54 acres.

4.   **b.** Colin's 3 acre lot contains 43,560 ft.^{2} /acre $\times 3 = 130{,}680$ ft.^{2}. Because the width of each lot is 120 ft. and there are 12 lots of equal with, the total width of Colin's lot is
120 ft. $\times 12 = 1{,}440$ ft. Therefore,
130,680 ft.$^2 = 1{,}440$ ft. $\times$ (depth of lot).
90.75 ft. $=$ depth of lot.

5.   **d.** Converting the dimensions into feet, each lot is 90 ft. deep and 121 ft. wide. Therefore, in the four lots there are 4×90 ft. $\times 121$ ft. $= 43{,}560 = 1$ acre.

6.   **a.** Since Section 2 contains 640 acres, the northwest quarter of Section 2 contains 160 acres and the west half of that parcel contains 80 acres. Similarly, the east half of Section 2 contains 320 acres, a quarter of that is 80 acres, and a quarter of that is 20 acres. Combining the two parcels, 80 acres + 20 acres, gives us 100 acres.

7.   **b.** Because 1 acre is 43,560 ft.^{2}, 3.5 acres $= 3.5 \times 43{,}560$ ft.$^2 = 152{,}460$ ft.^{2}

8.   **b.** A square yard is $3' \times 3' = 9$ ft.^{2}, so the lot is 300 yd.$^2 \times 9$ ft.^{2}/yd.$^2 = 2{,}700$ ft.^{2}. Since the frontage is 50 feet the depth is 2,700 feet $\div 50$ feet $= 54$ feet. <u>This question is an example of how important it is to convert all dimensions (i.e., yards, feet, etc.) stated in the problem to the same dimension before beginning your calculations.</u>

9.   **a.** Susan's 2-acre lot has $2 \times 43{,}560$ ft.$^2 = 87{,}120$ ft.^{2}. Therefore, each of the equal-size lots is 87,120 ft.$^2 \div 4 = 21{,}780$ ft.^{2}. 21,700 ft.$^2 \div 200$ ft. $= 108.9$ ft. width.

10.   **b.** Because a cubic yard is 3 ft. $\times 3$ ft. $\times 3$ ft. $= 27$ ft.^{3}, Brian is seeking to build a storage shed that is
50 yd.$^3 \times 27$ ft.^{3}/yd.$^3 = 1{,}350$ ft.^{3}. Therefore, 25 ft. $\times 6$ ft. $\times$ height $= 1{,}350$ ft.^{3}, so height $= 9$ ft.

11.   **a.** 58,080 yd.$^2 = 58{,}080$ yd.$^2 \times 9$ ft.^{2}/yd.$^2 = 522{,}720$ ft.^{2}
522,720 ft.$^2 \div 43{,}560$ ft.^{2}/acre $= 12$ acres.

12. **c.** Section A is a square having a base of 75 ft. and the height of 75 ft., so the area of section A is 75 ft. × 75 ft. = 5,625 ft.²

Section B is a rectangle having a base of 85 ft. and a height of 75 ft., so the area of section A is 85 ft. × 75 ft. = 6,375 ft.²

Section C is a triangle, in which the base = 90 ft. and the height = 75 ft. Therefore, the area of section C is ½ (90 ft. × 75 ft.) = 3,375 ft.², giving a total area of 5,625 ft.² + 6,375 ft.² + 3,375 ft.² = 15,375 ft.²

13. **a.** Let X stand for the price of lot A. Converting the word problem into an elementary algebraic statement, we have:
(cost of lot A) + (cost of lot B) = $124,000.
X + (X - $17,000) = $124,000.
2 X - $17,000 = $124,000.
2 X = $141,000
X = $70,500. Therefore, Amanda paid $70,500 - $17,000 = $53,500 for lot B.

14. **c.** By deconstructing the lot into three distinct sections, we see that section C is a square 50' × 50' = 2,500 ft.². Section B is a rectangle with a base of 200' and a height of 150', therefore having an area = 200' × 150' = 30,000 ft.². Section A has a base of 75'and a height of 100', therefore having an area of ½ (75' × 100') = 3,750 ft.². Hence, the area of A + B + C = 3,750 ft.² + 30,000 ft.² + 2,500 ft.² = 36,250 ft.².

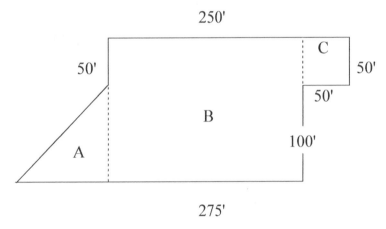

15. **d.** Because the shaded area extends into two distinct quarters of the section, we need to analyze each of the separate shaded areas separately. The smaller area is in the SE¼ of Section 8, is in the NE¼ of the SE¼ of Section 8, and is in the N½ of the NE¼ of the SE¼ of Section 8. The larger area is in the NE¼ of Section 8, and is in the SW¼ of the NE¼ quarter of Section 8.

CHAPTER 2: PERCENTAGES

Being able to work effectively with percentages is of vital importance to real estate agents, as well as to buyers and sellers of real estate, because nearly all real estate transactions involve several important percentage calculations, including calculations regarding commissions, profit, property taxes, interest rates, buyer-qualification ratios, loan-to-value ratios, capitalization rates, and percentage leases. In this chapter we will consider percentage problems related to commissions and profits, leaving other percentage problems to later chapters that are devoted to specific issues, such as mortgage, appraisal, and investment calculations.

A percentage (often expressed as a decimal) is a part of a whole, and is expressed as a rate (percent) multiplied by the amount of the whole. For example, in a commission split situation, a salesperson will want to know what how much of the commission earned by the employing broker the salesperson will receive. This salesman's share (percentage) of the commission will be calculated as a percent (such as 40% or 50%) of the commission received by the broker.

To convert a decimal to a percent, move the decimal point two places to the right and add the % sign:

.75 → 75%
1.12 → 112%

To convert a percent to a decimal, simply remove the % sign and move the decimal point two places to the left:

15% → .15
74.6% → .746

Example: There are 10,550 homes in a county. If 4% of those homes sold last year, how many homes in this county sold last year?

Answer: This question effectively asks: What part (what percentage) of the total number of homes in this county sold last year? To calculate this we convert 4% to .04 and multiply that number by the total number of homes: .04 × 10,550 = 422.

Example: During a hot real estate market, Sam sold his house for $168,000, which was a premium of 5% over asking (list) price. At what price was Sam's house listed?

Answer: This question asks: What part (what percentage) of the selling price was the list price? To calculate this, we convert 5% to .05 and translate the word problem written in English into the language of algebra, letting L stand for the list price:
$168,000 = L + (.05 × L)
       = 1.05 × L. Dividing both sides of the equation by 1.05, we get
$160,000 = L

Commission Calculations.

Because nearly every real estate agent expects to receive commissions (many, hopefully!), it is not unlikely that a question or two relating to commissions might appear on a real estate license exam. On the other side of this coin, of course, are buyers and sellers who must pay commissions and therefore should be able to calculate commissions as a part of the cost of their real estate transactions.

One of the most common commission problems on real estate exams — reflecting one of the most common real-world situations — involves commission splits among cooperating brokers and their respective salespersons. In these situations, cooperating brokers typically split the total commission received 50-50, and pay their respective salespersons a percent of what they receive. In such a situation, a salesperson receives a percent of a percent of the total commission paid, as in the following diagram:

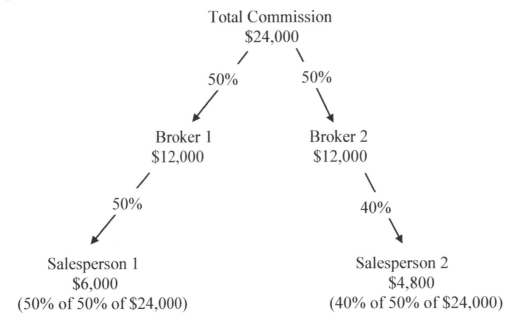

Example: Jessica is a real estate salesperson who found a buyer for a home that sold for $800,000. Jessica's employing broker received a 5% commission for the sale. The agreement between the broker and Jessica provides that she receive 40% of the broker's commission on every sale she procures. What is Jessica's commission on this transaction?

Answer: Here the solution is to first find the broker's commission:

5% of $800,000 = .05 × $800,000 = $40,000. Jessica is to receive 40% of $40,000 = .40 × $40,000 = $16,000.

Another way to think about such a problem is to note that Jessica receives 40% of 5% = .40 × .05 = .02 = 2% of the sales price. Using this 2% figure, we find that 2% of $800,000 = .02 × $800,000 = $16,000.

Example: Bob is a salesperson who works for broker Janet. Bob's agreement with Janet is that he gets a commission of 40% of whatever commission Janet receives on sales made by Bob. Bob procures a sale of a house that was listed by broker Susan, who had a cooperating agent agreement with Janet to split the commission on the sale 50-50. Susan's listing agreement with the owner called for a 6% commission. Bob's commission on the sale was $6,000. How much did the house sell for?

Answer: Because they tend to be long-winded, these types of problems *appear* to involve much more thought than they actually do — they simply need to be approached methodically, step-by-simple-step, until the answer falls out:

The problem tells us that:
$6,000 = 40% of 50% of 6% of Sales Price
   = (.4 × .5 × .06) × Sales Price
   = .012 × Sales Price (i.e., 1.2% of Sales Price)
Therefore, dividing each side of the equation by .012, we get
$500,000 = Sales Price.

Example: Ernesto sold his house, receiving $423,000 after paying a 6% commission. For how much did Ernesto sell his house?

Answer: We are told that the price the house sold for — its "Sales Price" — minus the commission paid was $423,000. Therefore,
Sales Price - Commission = $423,000
Sales Price - (6% of Sales Price) = $423,000
Sales price - (.06 × Sales Price) = $423,000
.94 × Sales Price = $423,000
Finally, dividing both sides of the equation by .94, we get
Sales Price = $450,000

Example: Emily is a salesperson who procured for her employing broker a listing for a house with list price of $395,000. The seller agreed to pay the broker a commission of 5% of the sales price. Emily's agreement with her broker is that she would receive 50% of any commission received by her broker coming from listings that she procures. With the help of a cooperating broker — who had a commission split agreement with Emily's employing broker whereby Emily's employing broker would receive 60% and the cooperating broker would receive 40% of the commission — the house eventually sold for 105% of the list price. What was Emily's commission on this transaction?

Answer: The house sold for 105% of $395,000 = 1.05 × $395,000 = $414,750. Therefore, the commission paid by the seller = 5% of $414,750 = 0.05 × $414,750 = $20,737.50. Emily's employing broker received 60% of this commission = 0.6 ×

$20,737.50 = $12,442.50. Emily received 50% of the commission received by her broker, which is $0.5 \times $12,442.50 = $6,221.25$.

Graduated Commission Splits

Some brokerages have adopted a **graduated commission split** contract, under which a salesperson's commission is based on the salesperson's achieving specified production goals, as in the next example.

Example: Kathy's contract with her employing broker states that for each transaction that Kathy handles, she will receive 50% of the broker's commission on the first $100,000 of the sales price, 60% of her broker's commission on the next $200,000, and 70% her broker's commission on any sales amount about $300,000. Kathy procured the sale of a home listed by her broker that sold for $280,000. The seller agreed to pay a 5% commission on the sales price. Her broker received his agreed 50-50 commission split with a cooperating broker. What was Kathy's commission on this transaction?

Answer: The total commission paid by the seller was 5% of $280,000 = $14,000. Kathy's broker received half of this amount, which is $7,000. Because the sales price was $280,000, we first have to calculate how much of the broker's $7,000 commission was due to the first $100,000 of the sales price and how much of the broker's commission was due to the next $180,000 of the sales price.
Broker's commission on the first $100,000 = 2.5% of $100,000 = $.025 \times $100,000 = $2,500.
Broker's commission on the next $180,000 = 2.5% of $180,000 = $.025 \times $180,000 = $4,500. Therefore,
Kathy's commission on the first $100,000 = 50% of $2,500 = $.5 \times $2,500 = $1,250.
Kathy's commission on the next $180,000 = 60% of $4,500 = $.6 \times $4,500 = $2,700. Therefore, Kathy's total commission on this sale is $1,250 + $2,700 = $3,950.

Profit and Loss Calculations.

Profit is defined as the gain realized when a property is sold for more than its cost (purchase price). *Loss*, on the other hand, is defined as the amount a property is sold for that is less than its cost. It is important when doing profit and loss calculations to keep in mind that both profit and loss — and rates of profit and loss — are based on the cost (purchase price) of the property, not on its selling price.

Example: Marvin sold his condo for $124,800, which was 4% more than he paid for the condo. How much did Marvin pay for his condo?

Answer: If we let P represent the purchase price of the condo, then
$$\$124,800 = P + 4\% \text{ of } P$$
$$= P + (.04 \times P)$$

= 1.04 × P. Dividing both sides of the equation by 1.04, we get $120,000 = P

Example: Let's look at the above example in a slightly different way. Suppose that Marvin sold his condo for $124,800 two years after he purchased it for $120,000, paying all cash. At what annual rate did Marvin profit from his investment?

Answer: Marvin's profit was $124,800 - $120,000 = $4,800. This profit was made over a period of two years, so his profit was $2,400 per year. Therefore, the annual rate at which he earned profit was $2,400 ÷ $120,000 = .02 = 2%. *It is important to note that to obtain this answer we did **not** divide $2,400 by the selling price because the rate of profit — or of loss — is relative to the purchase price, not to the selling price.*

Example: In January 2007 Betty purchased a house for $150,000. In January 2009, due to the severe real estate downturn and the loss of her job, she was forced to sell her home for $124,500. At what annual rate did Betty lose money on her house?

Answer: Betty's loss was $150,000 - $124,500 = $25,500. Because this loss occurred over a period of two years, Betty's annual loss was $12,750. Therefore, the annual rate of loss was $12,750 ÷ $150,000 = .085 = 8½ %.

Chapter 2 Quiz

Question 1: Brian has 23,500 homes in his sales area. Last year 4.6% of those homes were sold. How many homes were sold and Brian's area last year?

a. 1,081

b. 1,057

c. 1,058

d. 920

Question 2: Don sold his condo for $189,000, which was 10% under the list price. What was the list price of Don's condo?

a. $198,947 (rounded)

b. $170,100

c. $210,000

d. $207,900

Question 3: Benjamin wants to net $75,000 on the sale of his condo. Estimated closing costs are $5,000, and he agreed to a 5% broker's commission. What is the minimum price to condo must sell for to satisfy Benjamin?

a. $76,190 (rounded to the nearest dollar)

b. $78,947 (rounded to the nearest dollar)

c. $84,211 (rounded to the nearest dollar)

d. none of the above

Question 4: Susan sold her second home, receiving $313,500 after paying a 5% commission. What did Susan's second home sell for?

a. $333,000

b. $330,000

c. $297,825

d. none of the above

Question 5: The sale price of Emily's condo was $150,000. Emily paid $3,500 closing cost and a 5% commission. How much did Emily net from this sale?

a. $142,500

b. $139,175

c. $140,000

d. $139,000

Question 6: Kathy sold her house for $142,500, which was 5% less than the appraised price. What was the appraised price of Kathy's home?

a. $135,375

b. $150,000

c. $145,000

d. $144,750

Question 7: Sam is a salesperson who receives 50% of the commission on all commissions his employing broker, Bob, receives due to Sam's effort. Sam receives a commission of $8,450 due to his procurement of the sale of a house for which Bob had a 6% commission listing agreement. For how much did the house sell?

a. $140,833

b. $422,500

c. $280,000

d. none of the above

Question 8: Susan is a salesperson who sold a 1/4 acre lot for $17 per square foot. The commission rate her broker received was 8%, and Susan split the commission with her broker 50-50. How much did Susan earn on the sale?

a. $29,620.80

b. $14,810.40

c. $7,405.20

d. none of the above

Question 9: Julio sold a house for $475,000 and received $11,875 in commission. What commission rate did Julio receive on the sale?

a. 3%

b. 3.5%

c. 2%

d. none of the above

Question 10: After deducting a commission of 5% of the selling price, and closing costs of $7,300, Bob received $234,500, which was $4,650 less than he paid for the house a year earlier. How much did Bob pay for the house?

a. $242,260 (rounded to the nearest dollar)

b. $259,176(rounded to the nearest dollar)

c. $263,826(rounded to the nearest dollar)

d. $249,875(rounded to the nearest dollar)

Question 11: Olivia sold her condo and netted $85,000 from the sale. At the time of closing she had a mortgage with outstanding principal balance of $117,500. Closing costs were $5,450, and she paid a 5% commission on the sale. What was the selling price of Olivia's condo?

a. $207,950(rounded to the nearest dollar)

b. $202,500(rounded to the nearest dollar)

c. $213,445(rounded to the nearest dollar)

d. $218,895(rounded to the nearest dollar)

Question 12: Jessica bought her house for $200,000. Five years later she sold the house for $230,000. What percentage gross profit did she make on the sale?

a. 3%

b. 5%

c. 15%

d. 20%

Question 13: Kevin sold his mobile home for $64,800 four years after he purchased it for $60,000. At what annual rate did Kevin profit from his investment?

a. 1.85% (rounded)

b. 2%

c. 8%

d. 7.4% (rounded)

Question 14: Samuel sold his house and netted $50,000 from the sale. At the time of closing he had a mortgage with outstanding principal balance of $349,000. Closing costs were $4,750, and he paid a 5% commission on the sale. What was the selling price of Marvin's house?

a. $425,000

b. $403,750

c. $404,500

d. none of the above

Question 15: Amelia sold her condo for $220,000 and netted $45,000 from the sale. If Amelia's only costs related to the sale were the closing costs of $5,050 and the 5% commission she paid to her broker, what was Amelia's outstanding balance on her mortgage at the time of the sale?

a. $158,950

b. $159,000

c. $169,950

d. $164,000

Chapter 2 Quiz Answers

1.   **a.** 4.6% of 23,500 = .046 × 23,500 = 1,081

2.   **c.** \$189,000 = 90% of list price = .9 × list price. Dividing both sides the equation by .9, we get \$210,000.

3.   **c.** Let M represents the minimum price to condo must sell for to satisfy Benjamin.
M = \$75,000 + \$5,000 + (5% of M)
   = \$80,000 + .05 × M. Therefore,
.95 × M = \$80,000
M = \$84,211 (rounded)

4.   **b.** Let H stand for the selling price of Susan's second home. The problem tells us that
H = \$313,500 + (5% of H) = \$313,500 +.0 5H. Therefore,
.95 H = \$313,500
H = \$330,000

5.   **d.** The cost of the sale to Emily was
\$3,500 + 5% of \$150,000 = \$11,000. Therefore, Emily netted
\$150,000 - \$11,000 = \$139,000.

6.   **b.** Letting A stand for the appraised price, we translate the word problem as follows:
\$142,500 = A - (.05 × A).
         = .95 × A. Dividing both sides of the equation by .95, we get
\$150,000 = A.

7.   **d.** Sam effectively receives 3% of the sales he makes from Bob's listing. (Note that there would be no cooperating agent involved in a case such as this.) Therefore, if we let S stand for the sales price, \$8,450 = 3% of S = .03S. Then, dividing both sides of the equation by .03, we get \$8,450 ÷ .03 = \$281,667 (rounded).

8.   **c.** ¼ acre is 43,560 ft.² ÷ 4 = 10,890 ft.².
10,890 ft.² × \$17/ ft.² = \$185,130. Susan's commission was
50% of 8% of \$185,130 = 4% of \$185,130 = \$7,405.20

9.   **d.** \$11,875 ÷ \$475,000 = 0.025 = 2.5%

10.   **b.** Let Y stand for the price Bob sold the house for. The problem tells us that
Y = \$234,500 + \$7,300 + (.05 × Y).
   = \$241,800 + .05Y. Therefore, by subtracting .05Y from both sides of the equation, we get .95Y = \$241,800, so Y = \$241,800 ÷ .95 = \$254,526 rounded to the nearest dollar. Because this sales price represents a \$4,650 loss to Bob, Bob originally paid \$254,526 + \$4,650 = \$259,176 for the house.

11. **d.** Let P stand for the selling price of the condo. We know that P had to include the $85,000 that Olivia netted from the sale, the $117,500 mortgage balance, the $5,450 closing costs, and the commission, which we are told was 5% of P = .05 P. Hence,
P = $85,000 + $117,500 + $5,450 + .05 P. Subtracting .05 P from both sides of the equation and adding the amounts in the right side of the equation, we get
.95 P = $207,950. Dividing both sides of the equation by .95, we obtain
P = $218,895 (rounded to the nearest dollar)

12. **c.** She made $30,000 gross profit. $30,000 ÷ $200,000 = 15%. Note that the question does not ask for a *rate* of profit.

13. **b.** Kevin's profit was $64,800 - $60,000 = $4,800. Because this profit was made over a period of four years, Kevin's annual profit was $4,800 ÷ 4 = $1,200. Therefore, his annual rate of profit was $1,200 ÷ $60,000 = .02 equals 2%.

14. **a.** Let P stand for the selling price of the house. We know that P had to include the $50,000 that Marvin netted from the sale, the $349,000 mortgage balance, the $4,750 closing costs, and the commission, which we are told was 5% of P = .05 P. Hence, P = $50,000 + $349,000 + $4,750 + .05 P. Subtracting .05 P from both sides of the equation and adding the amounts in the right side of the equation, we get
.95 P = $403,750. Dividing both sides of the equation by .95, we obtain
P = $425,000.

15. **a.** Let M stand for the outstanding balance on Amelia's mortgage. Translating the word problem into the language of algebra, we obtain
$220,000 = $45,000 + $5,050 + (5% of $220,000) + M
= $50,050 + $11,000 + M. Subtracting $50,050 + $11,000 from both sides of the equation we get, $158,950 = M.

CHAPTER 3: MORTGAGE CALCULATIONS

A typical financial package for the purchase of real estate that involves a mortgage includes (1) a down payment; (2) a loan amount; (3) a calculation of interest paid throughout the term of the loan; (4) discount points; (5) origination fees; (6) some form of transfer tax (usually referred to as a documentary transfer tax, a stamp tax, a conveyance tax, or an intangible tax); (7) mortgage insurance; and (8) a schedule of monthly payments.

Interest.

Interest is the "rent" we pay to possess, use, and enjoy someone else's money. The yearly rent for each dollar we use (borrow) is determined by the interest rate — if the interest rate is 8% per year, we pay 8¢ each year for each dollar borrowed.

Interest problems generally involve four simple concepts:

1. *Interest Rate* (which, to avoid wordiness, we will call Rate);
2. *Principal* (the amount of money borrowed);
3. *Time* (the number of years or fraction of years the principal is borrowed);
4. *Interest Due and Owing* (which we will call Interest).

Because the interest due and owing (Interest) is equal to the interest rate (Rate) times the amount of money borrowed (Principal) times the amount of time the money is borrowed (Time),

Interest = Rate × Principal × Time

Example: What is the interest on $100,000 for one year if the rate of interest is 2.5%?

Answer: Using the formula Interest = Rate × Principal × Time,
Interest = .025/yr. × $100,000 × 1 yr. = $2,500.

Example: If the rate of interest on $10,000 is 6% per year and the loan is paid off in five months, how much interest would have been paid?

Answer: Using the formula Interest = Rate × Principal × Time,
Interest = .06/yr. × $10,000 × 5/12 yr. = $250

Example: What is the interest on $20,000 for four months if the rate of interest is 1.5%?

Answer: Using the formula Interest = Rate × Principal × Time,
Interest = .015/yr. × $20,000 × ⅓ yr. = $100.

The above interest formula is known as **simple interest**, which considers interest to be generated only on the principal invested. A more rapid method of generating interest earnings is referred to as compounding. **Compound interest** is generated when accumulated interest is reinvested to generate interest earnings from previous interest earnings. Though the amount of interest generated can be revved up by compounding yearly, semiannually, quarterly, daily, or even continuously, real estate exams stick with simple interest, as do most real estate loans on which interest is paid monthly.

When calculating interest problems, it is important to know what *day count convention* to use. An exact calculation would take into account the precise number of days: 30 days for some months, 31 or 28 or 29 for other months; 365 days for some years, 366 for leap years. In the days before computers, such calculations would have been quite burdensome, so the *30/360 day count convention* was adopted to simplify certain calculations. When using the 30/360 day count convention, each month is considered to have 30 days, and each year is considered to have 360 days. A year consisting of 360 days with 12 months of 30 days each is often referred to as a *statutory year*, or a *banker's year*. The 30/360 day count convention for calculating *interest*, *proration*, *insurance premiums*, and similar expenses is standard in the real estate market. However, in some areas, rules for calculating interest, proration, etc., are based on the actual number of days in a month or year. Interest calculated by the 30/360 day count convention is referred to as *ordinary interest*.

Interest questions and proration questions that appear on real estate exams will state whether calculations should be based on 360 or 365 days a year, and whether the day of closing belongs to the seller or to the buyer.

Example: If $6,000 is loaned for one 30-day month on the basis of simple interest, and the total amount of principal and interest due at the end of that month is $6,017.5, using the 30/360 day count convention, what annual rate of interest was charged?

Answer: Using the formula Interest = Rate × Principal × Time,
$17.50 = Rate × $6,000 × 1/12 year).
Therefore, annual interest rate = ($17.50 ÷ $6,000) × 12 = .035= 3.5%

Example: How much did Derek borrow at 5% if he paid $800 interest for a period of six months?

Answer: Using the formula Interest = Rate × Principal × Time,
$800 = 5%/yr. × Principal × 1/2yr. = .05/yr. × Principal × 1/2yr.
($800 ÷ .05/yr.) ÷ 1/2yr. = $32,000 = Principal
Example: What is the interest on a $400,000 loan for 1 year, 2 months, and 10 days at 6% interest (using a statutory year)?

Answer: The time elapsed is 360 days + 60 days +10 days = 430 days.
430 ÷ 360 = 1.19444 years. Therefore, applying our formula
Interest = Rate × Principal × Time, we get
Interest = .06/yr. × $400,000 × 1.19444 yr. = $28,666.67.

Example: Jessica borrows $12,000 from her friend Susan. The terms of the loan are that principal will be paid back in equal monthly installments over a five-year period along with the interest that was generated at the annual rate of 6% during the month on the outstanding balance of principal owing. What is Jessica's payment to Susan at the end of the second month, using the 30/360 day count convention?

Answer: To answer this question, we first have to answer another question; namely, how much principal does Jessica pay Susan at the end of the first month? This is due to the fact that Jessica's first month payment will reduce the principal amount on which the second month payment must be calculated.

Because there are 60 months in 5 years, the amount of Jessica's monthly payment attributable to principal is $12,000 ÷ 60 = $200. Therefore, the amount of principal owed after the first-month payment is made is $12,000 - $200 = $11,800. Consequently, the second month payment will be $200 + the interest due on $11,800 *for one month*. Because the interest rate is 6% annually, the monthly rate is 1/2%. Thus, the second-month payment is
$200 + 1/2% of $11,800 = $200 + .005 × $11,800 = $259.

Down Payment/Amount to Be Financed

A down payment is the amount of upfront money a lender requires a purchaser to pay toward the purchase price. Note that a down payment is what a lender requires; an earnest money deposit is what a seller requires. The two are different, though an earnest money deposit is often applied toward the down payment.

Example: Andrew is purchasing a home with a purchase price of $300,000 and an appraised value of $290,000. If the lender is willing to loan 80% of the lesser of the purchase price and the appraised value, how much will be Andrew's down payment?

Answer: Loan amount = $290,000 × .8 = $232,000.
Down payment = purchase price - loan amount
        = $300,000 - $232,000
        = $68,000.

Example: Margaret is purchasing a condo for $130,000. Her lender is requiring a 25% down payment. How much is the down payment that Margaret's lender is requiring?

Answer: 25% of $130,000 = .25 × $130,000 = $32,500.

Example: Brian's lender required a 20% down payment to obtain the mortgage on his house. The down payment amount was $55,000. What was the purchase price that Brian paid for his house?

Answer: 20% of the purchase price = .2 × (purchase price) = $55,000. Therefore, dividing both sides of the equation by .2, we get purchase price = $275,000.

Example: Kathy's lender is willing to loan 80% of the lesser of the purchase price of her condo and the condo's appraised value. The purchase price of the condo is $180,000. The loan amount is $132,000. What was the appraised value of the condo?

Answer: Because 80% of the purchase price ($180,000) = $144,000, but the loan amount was only $132,000, we know that the appraised value of the condo was less than the purchase price. In fact, we know that
80% of the appraised value of the condo = $132,000. Therefore,
the appraised value of the condo = $132,000 ÷ .8 = $165,000.

Loan-to-Value Ratios

The *loan-to-value ratio (LTV)* is an important risk factor lenders use to assess the viability of a proposed loan. LTV is typically calculated as the amount of a first mortgage divided by the *lesser* of (1) the appraised value of the property and (2) the purchase price of the property. As a general rule, a high LTV (usually seen as over 80%) will either cause:

- the loan to be denied;
- the lender to increase the cost of the loan to the borrower; or
- the lender to require that the borrower pay for private mortgage insurance.

Example: For a property with an appraised value of $100,000, a sales price of $110,000, and a loan of $90,000, what is the LTV if the LTV is based on the lesser of the appraised value or the sales price??

Answer: The lesser of (1) the appraised value of the property and (2) the purchase price of the property is $100,000. Therefore, LTV = $90,000/$100,000 = 90%.

Example: What is the required down payment on a $187,000 loan if the LTV is 85%?

Answer: If this were a question on an exam, because no mention is made of an appraised value versus the purchase price, we must assume that the LTV is based upon the purchase price.
LTV = .85 = $187,000 ÷ purchase price. Therefore,
purchase price = $187,000 ÷ .85 = $220,000.
Because in this case the down payment = purchase price - loan amount,
down payment = $220,000 - $187,000 = $33,000.

Example: If a loan has an LTV of 80%, the property has an appraised value of $120,000 and a sales price of $110,000, what is the amount of the loan if the LTV was based on the lesser of the appraised value or the sales price?

Answer: The lesser of (1) the appraised value of the property and (2) the purchase price of the property is $110,000. Therefore,
LTV = .8 = loan amount/$110,000.
Hence, loan amount equals $110,000 × .8 = $88,000.

Housing Affordability

Prior to approving a loan, a loan processor will obtain information on monthly housing expenses, which the underwriter will use to establish a ratio of monthly housing expenses to monthly gross income. The loan processor will also obtain information on total monthly recurring debt obligations, which the underwriter will use to establish a ratio of total monthly expenses to monthly gross income.

Monthly housing expenses include home-loan payments (principal plus interest), property taxes, and insurance (property insurance and private mortgage insurance). These monthly housing expenses are typically referred to as *PITI*, which is an acronym for **P**rincipal, **I**nterest, **T**axes, and **I**nsurance.

Total monthly expenses include housing expenses plus additional long-term monthly debt service, such as for car payments, credit card payments, child support, and alimony. In this context, "long-term debt" typically refers to debt that is not scheduled to be retired within 9 months. Monthly housing expenses divided by the monthly gross income is referred to as the *PITI ratio* or *front-end ratio*. Total monthly expenses divided by monthly gross income is referred to as the long-term debt ratio (*LTD ratio*) or *back-end ratio*.

Example: Suppose that

- monthly gross income = $4,000;
- monthly housing expenses = $1,000; and
- additional long-term monthly debt expenses = $400.

What are the PITI and LTD ratios?

Answer: In this case, PITI is $1,000 and LTD is $1,400.

- PITI ratio = $1,000 ÷ $4,000 = 25%
- LTD ratio = $1,400 ÷ $4,000 = 35%

A PITI of 25% and an LTD ratio of 35% will qualify for most loans, assuming that other elements of the borrower's loan application are within loan guidelines. Typically for conventional loans, a PITI ratio less than or equal to 28% and an LTD ratio less than or equal to 36% are required. FHA-insured and VA-guaranteed loans are usually a bit more lenient.

Example: Marcus wants to buy a condo. His gross monthly income is $3,500. His broker has informed him that his PITI ratio should not exceed 28% to qualify for the type of loan Marcus wants. Assuming the broker to be accurate, what are the maximum housing expenses Marcus can have to qualify for this type of loan on the basis of his income?

Answer: The maximum PITI ratio = 28%. Therefore,
.28 = maximum monthly housing expenses ÷ gross income

= maximum monthly housing expenses ÷ $3,500.
Multiplying both sides of the equation by $3,500, we get
$980 = maximum monthly housing expenses.

Example: Evan and Susan's monthly PITI payment is $1,218. Their lender required a PITI ratio of 28%. What is the minimum combined gross monthly income the lender required of Evan and Susan?

Answer: $1,218 ÷ (gross month income) = .28.
Therefore, gross monthly income = $1,218 ÷ .28 = $4,350.

Equity

Equity is the difference between the current market value of a property and the total indebtedness against the property. If each mortgage payment pays all of the current interest plus some part of the outstanding principal, then the equity increases with each mortgage payment in the amount of the outstanding principal reduction due to the mortgage payment.

Example: Suppose that you have a home with a fair market value $300,000, a first mortgage with outstanding principal of $200,000, and a home equity loan with outstanding principal of $27,000. What is the equity in your home?

Answer: The equity in your home would be $300,000 - ($200,000 + $27,000) = $73,000.

Example: If the equity in your home is $47,000 and its fair market value is $170,000, what is the total indebtedness against your home?

Answer: The equity in your home = fair market value - home's total indebtedness.
 Therefore, home's total indebtedness = home's fair market value - its equity.
Home's total indebtedness = $170,000 - $47,000 = $123,000

Home equity loans and home equity lines of credit (HELOC) are loans and lines of credit based on the equity of your home. However, when dealing with lenders and HELOCs, read carefully how "based on the equity of your home" is interpreted by the lender. Typically, these kinds of loans give a loan (or credit line) *up to 80% of the appraised value of your home, minus total outstanding indebtedness against the home, which is **not** equal to 80% of the equity in your home.*

Example: Joe's home is appraised at $200,000. The first mortgage against his home has an outstanding balance of $100,000, and there is no other indebtedness against his home. Joe has just arranged to obtain an 80% home equity line of credit of the type described above. What is the amount of his line of credit?

Answer: ($200,000 × .8) - $100,000 = $60,000.

Note that the answer is NOT ($200,000 - $100,000) × .8 = $80,000.

Private Mortgage Insurance (PMI)

Private mortgage insurance (PMI) is insurance that lenders often require for conventional loans with an LTV more than 80%. PMI *insurers the lender*, not the borrower, and *covers the top amount of the loan* (not the entire loan) in case of default.

Example: A property with a purchase price and an appraised value of $100,000 and a loan of $90,000 would have an LTV of 90%. If the lender required PMI to cover the top 20% of the loan, what would be the PMI coverage for the lender?

Answer: PMI covers the top amount of the loan — not the entire loan — in case of default. In this example, the lender requires the top 20% of the loan to be covered. 20% of $90,000 = $18,000.

Example: A lender has agreed to make a loan for a condo having a purchase price and an appraised value of $160,000. The loan has an LTV of 90%. If the lender required PMI to cover the top 20% of the loan, what would be the PMI coverage for the lender?

Answer: Because the LTV for this loan is 90%, the loan amount is .9 × $160,000 = $144,000. Therefore, the PMI coverage is 20% of $144,000 = $28,800.

Example: A lender has agreed to make a loan for a house having a purchase price and an appraised value of $400,000. The lender required PMI to cover the top 20% of the loan, which 20% turned out to be $68,000. What was the LTV of this loan?

Answer: We are told that 20% of the loan was $68,000. Therefore,
.2 × loan amount = $68,000. Therefore,
loan amount = $68,000 ÷ .2 = $340,000.
LTV = $340,000 ÷ $400,000 = .85 = 85%.

Example: Charles is putting 15% down on a house he is purchasing for $300,000. The lender is requiring an upfront payment of 1.25% of the loan amount for private mortgage insurance. How much must Charles deposit into escrow at the closing of this transaction?

Answer: In this example, Charles must deposit into escrow enough to cover both the down payment and the upfront PMI payment. The down payment is 15% of $300,000 = $45,000. Therefore, the amount of the loan is $300,000 - $45,000 = $255,000.
The upfront PMI payment = 1.25% of $255,000 = $3,187.50. Therefore, Charles must bring to escrow $45,000 + $3,187.50 = $48,187.50.

Mortgage Points

In finance, a *point* is equal to 1% of the loan amount. The term is used by lenders to measure discount charges and other costs such as origination fees and private mortgage insurance premiums.

Example: If 1.25 points are charged on a $150,000 loan, the lender would collect how much on these 1.25 points?

Answer: 1.25% of $150,000 = $1,875.

Example: If a lender charges 1.5 points on a loan, and the amount of this charge is $3,000, what was the amount of the loan?

Answer: We know that 1.5% of the loan amount = $3,000. Therefore, loan amount = $3,000 ÷ .015 = $200,000.

Discount points are a form of prepaid interest paid to a lender by a borrower to increase the lender's yield on loans that yield lower rates than investors currently demand, which is why discount points are sometimes referred to as *loan equalization factors*. One discount point is equal to 1% of the loan amount (not the purchase price). For example, if a borrower wished to obtain a loan rate 1% less than current market, a lender would charge the borrower a certain number discount points in order to make such a loan.

Example: Sally is purchasing a house for $250,000 with 20% down and has negotiated a very favorable interest rate. However, in order to obtain this favorable interest rate, the lender requires that Sally pay 2.5 discount points upfront. How much will Sally pay the lender for these discount points?

Answer: Sally is putting 20% of $250,000 = $50,000 down. Therefore, the loan amount is $250,000 - $50,000 = $200,000. The cost to Sally of the discount points would therefore be $200,000 × .025 = $5,000.

Historically, paying one discount point will reduce a borrower's mortgage rate by between .25% and .0125%, depending on the rate of interest. The higher the going rate of interest, the more discount points must be paid in order to reduce the mortgage rate by a given amount.

Example: Emily is purchasing a house for $300,000. She would like to obtain an interest rate lower than the going interest rate. In order to accommodate her wishes, her lender requires that she pay 2.5 discount points upfront. If the going rate of interest is such that paying one discount point reduces a borrower's mortgage by .25%, by how much is Emily able to reduce the interest rate on her loan by paying the required 2.5 discount points?

Answer: The simple answer to this long-winded problem is 2.5 discount points × .25%/discount point = .625%.

Example: A lender requires a yield on a loan to Sandra that is .5% greater than the interest rate on the loan quoted to Sandra. How many discount points must this lender charge Sandra in order to obtain the lender's required yield if to reduce the interest rate by .2% the lender must charge one discount point?

Answer: Since charging one discount point will raise the effective yield by .2%, the number of discount points needed are .5% ÷ .2% = 2.5 discount points.

Transfer Taxes

Most states, counties, and municipalities charge some form of transfer tax (usually referred to as a documentary transfer tax, a stamp tax, a conveyance tax, or an intangible tax) on the conveyance of properties.

Some states and local governments charge a transfer tax on real estate conveyances that is assessed only on the face value of the mortgage note. If the conveyance is financed in part by cash or by an assumed mortgage, this type of transfer tax would be assessed only on the value any the *new* mortgage note.

Example: Morgan takes out a loan to purchase a house with the sales price of $350,000. The amount of the mortgage note is 80% of the purchase price. If the intangible tax in Morgan's state is $1.50 for every $500 value of the note or fraction thereof, how much intangible tax would apply to this conveyance?

Answer: The amount of the mortgage note = $350,000 × 80% = $280,000.
$280,000 ÷ $500 = 560
560 × $1.50 = $840.

In addition to, or in lieu of, taxes on new mortgage notes as discussed above, state and local governments sometimes impose transfer taxes, typically on the recordation of deeds, based on the amount of consideration paid for the real property conveyed, exclusive of the value of any mortgage assumed. This type of transfer tax would be imposed on the value of any cash consideration paid for the property as well as on consideration paid from a new mortgage loan.

Example: Suppose your client is in a county that imposes a documentary transfer tax of $0.55 per $500 (or fraction thereof) on consideration paid for real property, exclusive of the value of any lien remaining on the property at the time of transfer. Suppose further that your client paid $100,000 cash, assumed a $250,000 mortgage, and took out a new mortgage in the amount of $75,000 for the purchase of a property. What would be the documentary transfer tax on this transfer?

Answer: In this case, the documentary transfer tax would be imposed on the value of the $100,000 cash and on the value of the $75,000 new mortgage. Therefore the documentary transfer tax would be ($175,000 ÷ $500) × $0.55 = 350 × $0.55 = $192.50.

Amortization

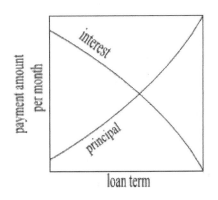

Installment loans require periodic payments that include some repayment of principal as well as interest. Installment loans are the most common type of loan used to finance real estate, and the most frequently used installment loan is the *level payment loan* — a loan under which all periodic installment payments are equal, though the amount allocated to principal and interest may vary over the term of the loan. A loan wherein the payments are sufficient to pay off the entire loan by the end of the loan term is referred to as a *fully amortized loan*. The accompanying diagram shows that with a level payment, fully amortized loan, during the first years of the loan term most of each month's payment goes to interest, but during the final years of the loan term most of each month's payment goes to reducing the principal. For a 30-year loan, the breakeven point occurs at 222 months (18.5 years) into the loan term.

Example: Elaine purchased a home for $225,000 with a 4% fixed-rate, fully amortized 30-year loan in the principal amount of $180,000. She makes payments of $859.50 per month. What is the amount of interest for the second month if calculated based on a 360-day year?

Answer: $180,000 × .04 ÷ 12 = $600 (first month's interest)
$859.50 - $600 = $259.5 (first month's principal payment)
$180,000 - $259.5 = $179,740.50 (principal balance after first month's payment).
$179,740.50 × .04 ÷ 12 = $599.14 (second month's interest, rounded).

Example: In the example immediately above, what is the total amount that Elaine will have paid when her loan is fully retired at the end of 30 years?

Answer: Elaine makes payments of $859.50 per month. She makes these payments for 12 months/year × 30 years = 360 months.
360 months × $859.50/month = $309,420, which is the total amount Elaine will have paid during the 30-year term of the loan.

Example: Referring to the two examples immediately above, what is the total amount of interest that Elaine will have paid when her loan is fully retired at the end of 30 years?

Answer: Because the original principal amount of the loan was $180,000, the total amount of interest paid during the term of the loan is
$309,420 - $180,000 = $129,420.

Amortization Charts

Although interest and principal payments for loans are now calculated on financial calculators or on calculation software freely available online, we will look briefly at a simplified amortization table to get a feel for how to calculate the monthly payments for fixed-rate, level payment loans at various interest rates.

The table displays in the left column the interest rate, and, in columns to the right, the term in years of a fixed-payment, fully amortized loan. To find the monthly payment *per $1,000* principal borrowed, simply find the intersection of the rate and term of the loan.

Monthly Payment Per $1,000 on Fixed-Rate, Level-Payment, Fully Amortized Loans				
Rate	10-year term	15-year term	30-year term	40-year term
4%	10.125	7.397	4.775	4.180
5%	10.607	7.908	5.369	4.822
6%	11.102	8.439	5.996	5.503
7%	11.611	8.989	6.653	6.215
8%	12.133	9.557	7.338	6.954

Example: Susan makes payments of $936 per month, including 6% interest on a fixed-rate, level-payment, fully amortized 30-year loan. What was the initial amount of her loan?

Answer: Finding where 6% and a 30-year term intersect in the table, we obtain the number 5.996 which is the dollar amount per month per $1,000 of the initial loan. $5.996/$1,000 = $936/loan amount. Therefore,
loan amount = ($936 ÷ $5.996) × $1,000 = $156,104.

Example: Margaret has a 5% fixed-rate, level-payment 15-year mortgage loan. The original amount of the loan was $200,000. What is Margaret's monthly mortgage payment?

Answer: Looking at the amortization table above, we see that the cell where the 5% row in the 15-year-term column intersect contains the number 7.908, which stands for the monthly dollar payment per thousand dollars principal borrowed. Because there were 200 thousand dollars borrowed, Margaret's monthly mortgage payment is $7.908 × 200 = $1,581.60.

Balloon Payments

A ***balloon payment*** is a mortgage payment, usually the final payment, that is significantly greater than prior payments — "significantly greater" generally being considered as being more than twice the lowest installment payment paid over the loan term.

Example: Your client wants to take out a 10-year, $300,000 straight loan at 4% interest. If interest payments are made in arrears monthly, what is the amount of the final (balloon) payment on this loan? (Note: A straight loan (also referred to as a term loan or an interest-only loan) is a loan under which periodic payments consist of interest only — the full amount of the principal being due at the end of the loan term in one lump sum.)

Answer: The annual interest is 4% of $300,000 = $12,000. Therefore, the monthly payment is $12,000 ÷ 12 = $1,000. The last payment on this loan would consist of the entire principal of $300,000 plus the $1,000 interest payment, which totals $301,000.

Prepayment Penalties

A prepayment penalty is a fee charged to a borrower for paying off a loan faster than scheduled payments call for. The penalty is usually calculated as a percentage of a certain number of months of interest on the loan.

Example: If a borrower has a $200,000 straight loan with interest at the rate of 4%, and the prepayment penalty the borrower incurs is 80% of six months interest, what is amount of the prepayment penalty?

Answer: The prepayment payment penalty would be 80% × 4%/year × ½ year × $200,000 = $3,200.

Chapter 3 Quiz

Question 1: What is the interest on $40,000 for three months if the rate of interest is 1.75%?

a. $700

b. $233.33

c. $175

d. $2,100

Question 2: If $10,000 is loaned for three months on the basis of simple interest, and the total amount of principal and interest due at the end of that month is $10,050 using the 30/360 day count convention, what annual rate of interest was charged?

a. ½%

b. 2%

c. 1.5%

d. none of the above

Question 3: What is the interest on a $200,000 loan for 1 year, 4 months, and 20 days at 4% interest (using the 30/360 day count convention)?

a. $10,888.89

b. $10,666.67

c. 10,444.44

d. $11,111.12

Question 4: If Oliver wishes to deposit enough money into a savings account that pays 3% annual interest to earn $1,000 each month, how much does he need to deposit into this account?

a. $33,333

b. $99,999

c. $400,000

d. none of the above

Question 5: A lender requires a yield on a loan to Billy that is .6% greater than the interest rate on the loan quoted to Billy. How many discount points must this lender charge Billy in order to obtain the lender's required yield if to reduce the interest rate by .15% the lender must charge one discount point?

a. 5 discount points

b. 4 discount points

c. 3 discount points

d. 2 discount points

Question 6: Jon financed his home with an 85% level-payment loan at a fixed annual rate of 5½%. Jon paid $3,895.83 interest the first month. How much did Jon pay for the house (rounded to the nearest dollar)?

a. $849,999

b. $722,499

c. $70,833

d. $999,999

Question 7: Joyce's lender is willing to loan 85% of the lesser of the purchase price of her house and the appraised value of the house. The purchase price of the house is $380,000. The loan amount is $318,750. What was the appraised value of the house?

a. $380,000

b. $323,000

c. $398,437.50

d. $375,000

Question 8: Your client takes out a loan to purchase a condo with the sales price of $145,000. The amount of the mortgage note is 80% of the purchase price. If the intangible tax in your state is $1.50 for every $500 value of the note or fraction thereof, how much intangible tax would apply to this purchase?

a. $145

b. $435

c. $174

d. $348

Question 9: Brian and Susan's monthly PITI payment is $2,184. Their lender required a PITI ratio of 28%. What is the minimum combined gross monthly income the lender required of Brian and Susan?

a. $7,800

b. $5,616

c. $3,602.94

d. none of the above

Question 10: John is purchasing a home with a purchase price of $235,000 and an appraised value of $225,000. If the lender is willing to loan 80% of the lesser of the purchase price and the appraised value, how much will be John's down payment?

a. $45,000

b. $55,000

c. $50,000

d. $40,000

Question 11: Example: If the rate of interest on a $20,000 straight loan is 9% per year and the loan is paid off in nine months, how much simple interest would have been paid? Use the 30/360 day count convention for your calculation.

a. $1,350

b. $1,800

c. $2,000

d. $675

Question 12: Example: John obtained a loan of $189,000, where the LTV was 90%. What was John's down payment?

a. $21,000

b. $18,900

c. $17,180

d. $20,000

Question 13: Stephen makes payments of $1,275 per month, including 4% interest on a fixed-rate, level-payment, fully amortized 15-year loan. Based on the amortization chart below, what was the initial amount of his loan, rounded to the nearest dollar?

Monthly Payment Per $1,000 on Fixed-Rate, Level-Payment, Fully Amortized Loans				
Rate	10-year term	15-year term	30-year term	40-year term
4%	10.125	7.397	4.775	4.180
5%	10.607	7.908	5.369	4.822
6%	11.102	8.439	5.996	5.503
7%	11.611	8.989	6.653	6.215
8%	12.133	9.557	7.338	6.954

a. $305,024

b. $267,016

c. $172,367

d. none of the above

Question 14: Tony has a 5% fixed-rate, level-payment 30-year mortgage loan. The original amount of the loan was $300,000. Referring to the amortization table in the question above, what is Tony's monthly mortgage payment?

a. $1,446.60

b. $2,372.40

c. $3,037.50

d. none of the above

Question 15: If a borrower has a $250,000 straight loan with interest at the rate of 5%, and the prepayment penalty the borrower incurs is 80% of six months interest, what is amount of the prepayment penalty?

a. $6,250

b. $5,000

c. $12,500

d. none of the above

Question 16: A lender is requiring a 25% down payment to obtain the mortgage on a house. The down payment amount is $43,750. What is the purchase price of the house?

a. $58,334

b. $131,250

c. $218,750

d. $175,000

Question 17: Alexi purchased a home for $390,260 with a 6% fixed-rate, fully amortized 30-year loan in the principal amount of $312,208. He makes payments of $1,872 per month. What is the total amount of interest that Alexi will have paid when his loan is fully retired at the end of 30 years?

a. $361,712

b. $283,660

c. $702,468

d. none of the above

Question 18: If a loan has an LTV of 90%, the property has an appraised value of $180,000 and a sales price of $160,000, what is the amount of the loan if the LTV was based on the lesser of the appraised value or the sales price??

a. $162,000

b. $172,000

c. $156,000

d. $144,000

Question 19: Emily is putting 10% down on a condo she is purchasing for $150,000. The lender is requiring an upfront payment of 1.75% of the loan amount for private mortgage insurance. How much must Emily deposit into escrow at the closing of this transaction?

a. $17,362.50

b. $17,625

c. $15,000

d. $12,637.50

Question 20: Margaret borrows $24,000 from her friend Janet. The terms of the loan are that principal will be paid back in equal monthly installments over a five-year period along with the interest that was generated at the annual rate of 3% during the month on the outstanding balance of principal owing. What is Margaret's payment to Janet at the end of the second month, using the 30/360 day count convention?

a. $59

b. $708

c. $459

d. $1,108

Question 21: George wants to buy a house. His gross monthly income is $6,500. His broker has informed him that his PITI ratio should not exceed 28% to qualify for the type of loan George wants. What are the maximum housing expenses George can have to qualify for this type of loan on the basis of his income?

a. $4,680

b. $2,860

c. $1,820

d. $2,059.20

Question 22: Cory purchased a home for $262,500 with a 5% fixed-rate, fully amortized, 30-year loan in the principal amount of $210,000. He makes payments of $1,127.49 per month. What is the amount of interest for the second month if calculated based on a 360-day year?

a. $780.52 (rounded to the nearest cent)

b. $875.00 (rounded to the nearest cent)

c. $873.95 (rounded to the nearest cent)

d. none of the above

Question 23: Amanda purchased as a home in a county that imposes a documentary transfer tax of $0.55 per $500 (or fraction thereof) on consideration paid for real property, exclusive of the value of any lien remaining on the property at the time of transfer. Amanda paid $50,000 cash, assumed a $350,000 mortgage, and took out a new mortgage in the amount of $85,250 for the purchase of the home. What would be the documentary transfer tax on this purchase?

a. $148.50

b. $534.05

c. $149.05

d. $533.50

Question 24: Roberto is purchasing a house for $450,000 with 20% down and has negotiated a very favorable interest rate. However, in order to obtain this favorable interest rate, the lender requires that Roberto pay 1.5 discount points upfront. How much will Roberto pay the lender for these discount points?

a. $6,750

b. $540

c. $5,400

d. $675

Question 25: Blake's home has a fair market value of $400,000. The total outstanding indebtedness against his home is $310,000. Blake has just arranged to obtain a home equity line of credit in an amount equal to 80% of the value of his home, minus the total outstanding indebtedness against the home. What is the amount of his line of credit?

a. $72,000

b. $10,000

c. $320,000

d. $248,000

Chapter 3 Quiz Answers

1.   c. Using the formula Interest = Rate × Principal × Time,
Interest = .0175/yr. × $40,000 × ¼yr. = $175.

2.   b. Using the formula Interest = Rate × Principal × Time,
$50 = Rate/yr. × $10,000 × ¼ yr.
$50 ÷ ¼yr. ÷ $10,000 = Rate/yr.
.02/yr. = 2%/yr. = Rate/yr.

3.   d. The time elapsed is 360 days + 120 days +20 days = 500 days.
500 ÷ 360 = 1.38889 years. Therefore, applying our formula
Interest = Rate × Principal × Time, we get
Interest = .04/yr. × $200,000 × 1.38889 yr. = $11,111.12.

4.   c. Oliver wants to earn interest at the rate of $12,000 per year, so
$12,000 = 3%/yr. × Principal × 1 yr. = .03 × Principal.
$12,000 ÷ .03 = Principal = $400,000.

5.   b. Since charging one discount point will raise the effective yield by .15%, the number of discount points needed are .6% ÷ .15% = 4 discount points.

6.   d. Because we are dealing with a level payment loan, the interest on the first month would be the monthly interest paid on the full amount of loan, which is
($3,895.83 × 12) ÷ .055= $849,999.27, which
represents 85% of the cost of the house. Therefore, the cost
of the house is $849,999.27 ÷ 85% = $999,999 (rounded).

7.   d. Because 85% of the purchase price ($380,000) = $323,000, but the loan amount was only $318,750, we know that the appraised value of the house was less than the purchase price. In fact, we know that
85% of the appraised value of the house = $318,750. Therefore,
the appraised value of the house = $318,750 ÷ .85 = $375,000.

8.   d. The amount of the mortgage note = $145,000 × 80% = $116,000.
$116,000 ÷ $500 = 232
232 × $1.50 = $348.

9.   a. $2,184 ÷ (grossly month income) = .28.
Therefore, gross monthly income = $2,184 ÷ .28 = $7,800.

10.   b. Loan amount = $225,000 × .8 = $180,000.
Down payment = purchase price - loan amount
            = $235,000 - $180,000

= $55,000.

11. **a.** Using the formula Interest = Rate × Principal × Time,
Interest = .09/yr. × $20,000 × 9/12 yr. = $1,350.

12. **a.** Because no mention is made of an appraised value versus the purchase price, we must assume that the LTV is based upon the purchase price.
LTV = .90 = $189,000 ÷ purchase price. Therefore,
purchase price = $189,000 ÷ .90 = $210,000.
Because in this case the down payment = purchase price - loan amount,
down payment = $210,000 - $189,000 = $21,000.

13. **c.** Finding where 4% and a 15-year term intersect in the table, we obtain the number $7.397 which is the dollar amount per month per $1,000 of the initial loan.
$7.397/$1,000 = $1,275/loan amount. Therefore,
loan amount = ($1,275 ÷ $7.397) × $1,000 = $172,367.

14. **d.** Referring to the amortization table, we see that the cell where the 5% row in the 30-year-term column intersect contains the number 5.369, which stands for the monthly dollar payment per thousand dollars principal borrowed. Because there were 300 thousand dollars borrowed, Tony's monthly mortgage payment is 5.369 × 300 = $1,610.70.

15. **b.** The prepayment payment penalty would be 80% × 5%/year × ½ year × $250,000 = $5,000.

16. **d.** 25% of the purchase price = .25 × (purchase price) = $43,750. Therefore, dividing both sides of the equation by .25, we get purchase price = $175,000.

17. **a.** Alexi makes payments of $1,872 per month. He makes these payments for 12 months/year × 30 years = 360 months.
360 months × $1,872/month = $673,920, which is the total amount Alexi will have paid during the 30-year term of the loan. Because the original principal was $312,208, the total amount of interest paid during the term of the loan is $673,920 - $312,208 = $361,712.

18. **d.** The lesser of (1) the appraised value of the property and (2) the purchase price of the property is $160,000. Therefore,
LTV = .9 = loan amount/$160,000.
Hence, loan amount equals $160,000 × .9 = $144,000.

19. **a.** In this example, Emily must deposit into escrow enough to cover both the down payment and the upfront PMI payment. The down payment is

10% of $150,000 = $15,000. Therefore, the amount of the loan is
$150,000 - $15,000 = $135,000.

The upfront PMI payment = 1.75% of $135,000 = $2,362.50. Therefore, Emily must bring to escrow $15,000 + $2,362.50 = $17,362.50.

20.   **c.** Because there are 60 months in 5 years, the amount of Margaret's monthly payment attributable to principal is $24,000 ÷ 60 = $400. Therefore, the amount of principal owed after the first-month payment is made is $24,000 - $400 = $23,600. Consequently, the second month payment will be $400 + the interest due on $23,600 *for one month*. Because the interest rate is 3% annually, the monthly rate is 1/4%. Thus, the second-month payment is

$400 + 1/4% of $23,600 = $400 + .0025 × $23,600 = $459.

21.   **c.** The maximum PITI ratio = 28%. Therefore,

.28 = maximum monthly housing expenses ÷ gross income

   = maximum monthly housing expenses ÷ $6,500.

Multiplying both sides of the equation by $6,500, we get

$1,820 = maximum monthly housing expenses.

22.   **c.** $210,000 × .05 ÷ 12 = $875 (first month's interest)

$1,127.49 - $875 = $252.49 (first month's principal payment)

$210,000 - $252.49 = $209,747.51 (principal balance after first month's payment).

$209,747.51 × .05 ÷ 12 = $873.95 (second month's interest, rounded).

23.   **c.** In this case, the documentary transfer tax would be imposed on the value of the $50,000 cash and on the value of the $85,250 new mortgage. Therefore, in this case, the "new money" subject to the documentary transfer tax would be

$50,000 (cash) + $85,250 (new mortgage) = $135,250.

$135,250 ÷ $500 = 270.5. Because this county imposes a documentary transfer tax of $0.55 per $500, **or fraction thereof**, the documentary transfer tax would be 271 × $0.55 = $149.05.

24.   **c.** Roberto is putting 20% of $450,000 = $90,000 down. Therefore, the loan amount is $450,000 - $90,000 = $360,000. The cost to Roberto of the discount points would therefore be $360,000 × .015 = $5,400.

25.   **b.** ($400,000 × .8) - $310,000 = $10,000. Note that this is *not* 80% of the equity in his home.

CHAPTER 4: REAL ESTATE TAXES

Property taxes are the main source of revenue for most local governments. Property taxes are ***ad valorem*** taxes, meaning that these taxes vary in proportion to the value of the property taxed. The value used is not necessarily the fair market value; rather, it is the ***taxable value***.

Tax Rates

The taxable value of a property is the ***assessed value*** (the value assessed, usually by the county or city assessor) of the property minus any exemption permitted by state and local laws (such as a homestead exemption, a veteran's exemption, a disabilities exemption, or a senior citizen exemption). Thus,

Taxable Value = Assessed Value - (Applicable Exemptions).

To find the annual property tax, take the taxable value and multiply by the annual ***tax rate***.

Annual Property Tax = Taxable Value × Annual Tax Rate

Depending on state and local custom, the annual property tax rate is expressed in different ways:

1) as a percentage;
2) as mills (a mill is 1/1000 of a dollar or $.001/$1); or
3) as dollars per $100.

	Equivalent Expressions of Property Tax Rates		
	% Rate	Mill Rate	Dollars per Hundred
County	1.2%	12 mills	$1.20
City	.15%	1.5 mills	$0.15
Total	1.35%	13.5 mills	$1.35

Example: John owns a single-family house that he rents to his cousin. The assessed value on the house is $275,000, and no exemptions apply. The annual property tax rate is 1.25%. What is the annual property tax on this house?

Answer: 1.25% of $275,000 = $3,437.50

Example: Andrew's vacant lot has a fair market value of $50,000. The assessed value of Andrew's lot is 60% of its fair market value. The annual property tax mill rate is 25. What is the annual property tax on Andrew's lot?

Answer: Because this example does not indicate that any property tax exemptions apply (which is typical for vacant lots), we must assume that the taxable value is the assessed value, which we are told is 60% of $50,000 = $30,000. The tax rate is 25 mill = $25/$1,000; therefore, the annual property tax on Andrew's lot is $25/$1,000 × $30,000 = $750.

Example: An apartment building has an assessed value of $2,327,000, and no exemptions apply. The annual property tax rate is $1.20 per hundred ($1.20/$100). What is the annual property tax on this apartment building?

Answer: $1.20/$100 × $2,327,000 = $27,924.

The most common property-tax exemption seen on real estate exams is the homestead exemption. A *homestead* is a family's place of residence. Most states have enacted homestead laws that exempt from property taxation a certain dollar amount — often dependent upon whether the property is owned by a single person, a married couple, or a senior citizen.

Example: A home has a fair market value of $450,000. The only applicable exemption is a homestead exemption of $75,000. The home has an assessed value of $368,000, and an annual county property tax of 1.2%. What is the taxable value of this home?

Answer: Taxable Value = Assessed Value - Homestead Exemption
$$= \$368,000 - \$75,000$$
$$= \$293,000.$$

Example: In the above example, what is the annual county property tax on this home?

Answer: $293,000 × .012 = $3,516.

Example: In the above example, what is the amount of tax savings due to the homestead exemption?

Answer: $75,000 × .012 = $900.

Special Assessments

Certain laws lay the groundwork for significant increases in taxes on property by permitting local governments to tax property for "special benefits" conferred on properties in particular limited areas. There are many such *special assessments* (also referred to as *impact fees*) for such items as streets, sewers, lighting, water service, parks, playgrounds, tree planting, landscaping, parking facilities, geologic hazard abatement, and so on. Special assessments attach special assessment liens only on the properties "benefited" in particular areas and are therefore specific liens.

For example, if a city extends sewer lines to a newly developed subdivision, such improvements benefit the owners of the subdivision parcels, not the public at large, and the cost of such improvements would be met by special assessment liens being placed against the owners of the subdivision parcels. Or, if sidewalks in a particular neighborhood are improved, the streets are lined with new trees, and new street lights are installed, such improvements also primarily benefit the homeowners of the neighborhood, and the cost of the improvements would be apportioned to the homeowners based on the footage of each property (not on the value of the property — special assessments are not ad valorem taxes).

However, if the streets of a neighborhood are widened to provide for increased commuter traffic, such improvements would primarily benefit the public, and the cost of such improvements would be borne by the public — including payment to the homeowners in the neighborhood for loss of land pursuant to eminent domain laws.

Finally, in some cases — such as the paving of unpaved streets or the repaving of potholed streets — a city or county may assess properties fronting the streets with only a percentage of the improvement costs because it is determined that the public at large is also significantly benefited by such improvements.

Example: Sidewalks in Amber's neighborhood are replaced at a cost of $15 per linear foot of sidewalk, which cost is being assessed 100% to the homeowners along the street. Amber's property is 15,000 ft.² and has a depth of 150 ft. What will be the special assessment made against Amber's property?

Answer: The assessment will be made based on the frontage of Amber's property. Because the area of her property is 15,000 ft.² and the depth of the property is 150 ft., her frontage is 15,000 ft.² ÷ 150 ft. = 100 ft.
100 ft. × $15/ft. = $1,500.

Example: Marjorie lives on unpaved street in an area recently annexed by a city. The city intends to pave the street and to assume 50% of the paving cost, assessing the remaining 50% to the homeowners having frontage along the street. The paving costs are anticipated to be $47 per linear foot of street. Marjorie's frontage is 95 feet. What is the amount of special assessment apportioned to Marjorie's property?

Answer: The paving cost of the portion of street along Marjorie's property is $47/ft. × 95/ft. = $4,465. However, the city is paying 50% of the paving cost, which is .5 × $4,465 = $2,232.50. Additionally, because there are two sides to the street, Marjorie's property would pay only ½ of the per-street-foot cost, so Marjorie's property would be assessed .5 × $2,232.50 = $1,116.25.

Note: In the prior example regarding Amber's property, the problem stated that the cost was $15 per foot of sidewalk, not per linear foot of street, so there was no 50% assessment reduction made.

Chapter 4 Quiz

Question 1: Margaret's home has a fair market value of $450,000, a homestead exemption of $100,000, an assessed value of $348,000, and a county property tax of 1.2%. What is the annual county property tax on this home?

a. $5,400

b. $4,200

c. $4,176

d. none of the above

Question 2: A home has a fair market value of $275,000, a homestead exemption of $75,000, an assessed value of $250,000, a county property tax of 1.2%, and a city property tax of .75%. What is the annual property tax on this home?

a. $2,100

b. $3,412.50

c. $5,362.50

d. $3,300

Question 3: Amelia's home has a fair market value of $650,000, a homestead exemption of $125,000, an assessed value of $475,000, a county property tax of 1.2%, and a city property tax of .75%. What is the amount of city property tax savings due to the homestead exemption?

a. $6,825

b. $2,625

c. $562.50

d. $937.50

Question 4: A vacant lot has a fair market value of $85,000. The assessed value of the lot is 30% of its fair market value. The annual property tax mill rate is 45. What is the annual property tax on this lot?

a. $11,475

b. $3,825

c. $3,442.50

d. none of the above

Question 5: Trees are planted along both sides of the streets in John's neighborhood at a cost of $10 per linear foot. The cost of this tree planting is being assessed 100% to the homeowners along the street. John's property is 8,000 ft.² and has a depth of 100 ft. What will be the special assessment made against John's property?

a. $1,000

b. $500

c. $800

d. $350

Question 6: Elaine lives on unpaved street in an area recently annexed by a city. The city intends to pave the street and to assume 70% of the paving cost, assessing the remaining 30% to the homeowners having frontage along the street. The paving costs anticipated to be $50 per linear foot of street. Elaine frontage is 125 feet. What is the amount of special assessment apportioned to Marjorie's property?

a. $656.25

b. $2,187.50

c. $937.50

d. $1,031.25

Chapter 4 Quiz Answers

1. **d.** ($348,000 - $100,000) × .012 = $2,976.

2. **b.** ($250,000 - $75,000) × (.012 + .0075) = $3,412.50.

3. **d.** Here, we are concerned with the city tax only, so $125,000 × .0075 = $937.50.

4. **d.** Because no property tax exemption is indicated, we must assume that the taxable value is the assessed value, which we are told is 30% of $85,000 = $25,500. The tax rate is 45 mill = $45/$1,000; therefore, the annual property tax on the lot is $45/$1,000 × $25,500 = $1,147.50.

5. **c.** The assessment will be made based on the frontage of John's property. Because the area of his property is 8,000 ft.² and the depth of the property is 100 ft., his frontage is 8,000 ft.² ÷ 100 ft. = 80 ft. $10/ft. × 80 ft. = $800.

6. **c.** The paving cost of the portion of street along Elaine's property is $50/ft. × 125/ft. = $6,250. However, the property owners are only paying for 30% of the paving costs, and, because there are two sides to the street, Elaine's property would pay only ½ of the per-street-foot cost, so Elaine's property would be assessed $6,250 × .3 × .5 = $937.50.

CHAPTER 5: VALUATION OF, AND INVESTING IN, PROPERTY

One of the most important characteristics of property, real or personal, is its value. Because the value of property lies at the heart of the real estate business, real estate agents should have a good grasp of the theoretical concepts of value and of the appraisal process. As a real estate agent, you will constantly be asked by clients what you think is the market value or rental value of their property.

Market Value and Market Price:

Market value is defined for appraisal purposes by HUD/FHA as: *"The most probable price which a property should bring in a competitive and open market under all conditions requisite to a fair sale, the buyer and seller each acting prudently, knowledgeably and assuming the price is not affected by undue stimulus."*

Market value is a distinct concept from market price. *Market price* is the price actually paid for a particular property, which might not have been the "most probable price" that the property "should bring" in a competitive and open market with buyers and sellers acting "knowledgeably" and "prudently."

Methods of Estimating Value/Appraisal Process

There are three main appraisal approaches that may be considered, and if necessary reconciled, in making a market valuation of a property:

1. *Market or Sales Comparison Approach* — compares recent sales of similar properties in the area to evaluate the market value of the subject property.

2. *Replacement Cost or Summation Approach* — obtains the market value of the subject property by adding the value of the land (unimproved) of the subject property to the depreciated value of the cost (if purchased at current prices) of the improvements on the subject property.

3. *Income Approach* — determines the market value of the subject property by capitalizing the estimated future income of the property.

Market or Sales Comparison Approach

The market or sales comparison approach (also known as the *market data approach*) is the best method for appraising land, residences, and other properties for which there is a ready market of similar properties. It is based on what is referred to as the *principle of substitution*, which holds that buyers are generally unwilling to pay more for a property than for a substitute property in the area. Using this method, the appraiser gathers data on recent sales (if sold at fair market value) of comparable properties in the area and makes comparisons of each of the features of the comparable properties to arrive at an estimate of the current market value of the subject property.

Once these data are collected, the appraiser adjusts the sales price of the comparable properties by *estimating what these properties would have sold for if they had had the same features as the subject property*. A **comparable property** is a property similar to the subject property that recently sold at arm's length, where neither the buyer nor the seller was acting under significant financial pressure. Note that it is the value of the similar features of the comparable properties that are adjusted, not the value of the features of the subject property. If a feature of a comparable property is *superior* to the same type of feature of the subject property, then an adjustment equal to the estimated difference in value of the feature of the comparable property to the feature of the subject property is *subtracted* from the comparable. If, on the other hand, the feature of the comparable property is *inferior* to the same type of feature of the subject property, then the estimated difference between the value of that feature of the subject property and the feature of the comparable is *added* to the comparable.

Example of Sales Comparison Approach

Assume that the subject property is a 2,200 ft.², 10-year-old, single-family home in good condition, with a good view, 3 bedrooms, 3 baths, and a 2-car garage. Assume also that there has been no appreciation in home values since the dates of the sales of the three comparables.

	Comparable 1	Comparable 2	Comparable 3	Subject
sales price	$850,000	$920,000	$880,000	?
condition	equal	equal	equal	good
view adjustment	inferior* + $5,000	superior* - $2,000	equal	good
age	equal	equal	equal	10 years old
square footage adjustment	equal	superior*(2,250) - $50,000	equal	2,200
bedrooms	equal	equal	equal	3
baths adjustment	inferior*(2 ½) + $5,000	equal	superior*(3½) - $5,000	3
garage	equal	equal	equal	2
Net adjustment	+ $10,000	- $52,000	- $5,000	
Adjusted sale price	$860,000	$868,000	$875,000	
Indicated value				$870,000

*Inferior means that the comparable's feature is inferior to the same feature of the subject property. Superior means the opposite. A subtraction of value is estimated if the comparable feature is superior; an addition of value if inferior.

Reconciliation: Comparable 3 is the most similar to the subject property, so its adjusted value is given slightly more weight. Indicated value: $870,000.

Example: The subject property and a comparable property are virtually identical except that the comparable as an inferior view estimated to be worth $2,500 less than the subject view, and the comparable has superior landscaping estimated to be worth $1,000 more than the subject landscaping. What adjustments should be made?

Answer The comparable has a view and landscaping combined value of $1,500 *less* than the subject view and landscaping value. Therefore, the comparable value should be *adjusted up* by $1,500.

Example: The subject property and a comparable are similar homes except that the comparable as an inferior view estimated to be worth $500 less than the subject view, and the comparable has superior landscaping estimated to be worth $1,000 more than the subject landscaping. What adjustments should be made?

Answer The comparable has a view and landscaping combined value of $500 *more* than the subject view and landscaping value. Therefore, the comparable value should be *adjusted down* by $500.

Example: What would be the estimated market value of a subject lot measuring 100' × 130' if the following 3 comparables are used for the analysis?
Comparable 1: Measures 100' × 110', sold for $99,000.
Comparable 2: Measures 120' × 130', sold for $132,600.
Comparable 3: Measures 110' × 130', sold for $135,850

a. $138,000

b. $140,000

c. $150,000

d. none of the above

Answer: d. Comparable 1: 100' × 110' = 11,000 sq. ft.
$99,000 ÷ 11,000 sq. ft. = $9/sq. ft.
Comparable 2: 120' × 130' = 15,600 sq. ft.
$132,600 ÷ 15,600 sq. ft. = $8.50/sq. ft.
Comparable 3: 110' × 130' = 14,300 sq. ft.
$135,850 ÷ 14,300 sq. ft. = $9.5/sq. ft.
($9 + $8.5 + $9.5) ÷ 3 comparables = $9/sq. ft.
Estimated value of subject property: 100' × 130'= 13,000 sq. ft.
13,000 sq. ft. × $9/sq. ft. = $117,000.

Replacement Cost or Summation Approach

The replacement cost or summation approach calculates the value of a subject property by:

1. **Estimating the value of the land as if vacant.** This step is usually performed using the sales comparison approach.

2. **Estimating the cost of replacing (or reproducing) the improvements.** This step involves first deciding whether to use replacement cost or reproduction

cost. ***Reproduction cost*** is the cost of replacing the improvements with exact replicas at current prices. ***Replacement cost*** is the cost of replacing the improvements with those having equivalent utility, but constructed with modern materials, designs, and workmanship. If a building is quite old, it likely was built with materials that are now quite expensive and that were installed with detailed hand-labor. In such a case, reproduction cost would not, in general, represent the current market value of the building, so the appraiser would use replacement cost in the appraisal.

There are four primary methods used to estimate reproduction or replacement cost:

- the most widely used method is the ***square-foot method***, which involves collecting cost data on recently constructed similar buildings and dividing the total cost by the square footage to obtain cost per square foot;

- the ***quantity survey method*** is the most detailed method, in which an estimate is made of the cost of all of the raw materials needed to replace the building. Such material-cost information is available in construction cost handbooks;

- the ***unit-in-place method*** estimates the unit cost of components of the structure;

- the ***cubic-foot method*** is much like the square-foot method except that it uses the volume of recently constructed similar buildings. This method often is used for warehouses and other industrial buildings.

3. **Subtracting the accrued depreciation of the improvements.** ***Accrued depreciation*** is depreciation that has happened prior to the date of valuation. By contrast, ***remainder depreciation*** is depreciation that will occur after the date of valuation. The two most used methods of calculating accrued depreciation are the straight-line method and the cost-to-cure method.

- **Straight-line method of calculating depreciation.** The ***straight-line method*** (also referred to as the ***age-life method***) calculates the amount of annual depreciation by dividing the cost of the improvement by the estimated ***useful life*** (***economic life***) of a typical such improvement. Once the cost and the useful life of an improvement have been determined, calculating the straight-line depreciation is easy, as illustrated in the following example.

  Example: If an improvement had a cost of $1,000,000 and a typical such improvement had a useful life of 50 years (with no residual value), what would be the annual appreciation rate according to the straight-line method?

  Answer: The straight-line method would determine the annual depreciation to be $1,000,000 ÷ 50 = $20,000, which is a depreciation rate of 2% per year.

  Example: In reference to the example above, an appraiser would next estimate the ***effective age*** of the improvement, which is defined as the age that is indicated by the condition of the structure, as distinct from its chronological age. If, in this example, the appraiser determined that the effective age of the improvement was 10 years rather than its chronological age of 20 years (perhaps because of greater than average care and upkeep), what would be the accrued depreciation?

Answer: The accrued depreciation would be $20,000 × 10 = $200,000 (rather than $20,000 × 20).

- **Cost-to-cure method of calculating depreciation.** The *cost-to-cure method* calculates depreciation by estimating the cost of curing the curable depreciation and adding to it the value of the incurable depreciation.

Example: A building depreciates by 2% per year. How many years will it take for the building to be worth only 40% of its initial value?

Answer: It takes 60 ÷ 2 = 30 years to depreciate by 60%, leaving 40% value.

Example: George sold a building for $1,250,000 that he had purchased 5 years earlier for $1,350,000. What was the average annual rate of depreciation (loss in value) of the building?

Answer 3: Loss = $1,350,000 - $1,250,000 = $100,000.
Average annual loss = $100,000 ÷ 5 years = $20,000/yr.
$20,000/yr. ÷ $1,350,000 = 1.48% per year.

Example: Martha purchased a building for $2,000,000 that had a useful life of 30 years and an anticipated residual value of $500,000. After 10 years, what is the value of the building, if by "value" we mean the original cost less accumulated straight-line depreciation?

Answer: Annual depreciation = (cost of property - residual value) ÷ useful life of property.
Therefore, annual depreciation = ($2,000,000 - $500,000) ÷ 30 = $50,000.
Accumulated straight-line depreciation equals $50,000 × 10 = $500,000.
$2,000,000 - $500,000 = $1,500,000.

The cost approach is likely to be the approach of choice if (1) there are few if any comparables in the area (thus eliminating the sales-comparison approach) and the income approach is inappropriate, or (2) the improvements are quite new so that data on precise current costs can be gathered. The older the improvement, the less likely it is that an estimate of replacement cost can be made with precision. Furthermore, replacement cost would not take into consideration changes in the neighborhood, zoning laws, etc. that would have occurred in the meanwhile. Therefore, appraising a 50-year old house using the cost method would likely result in an unrealistic appraisal.

Example of Cost Approach

Assume that the subject property is a 50 ft. x 40 ft. rectangular single-story house with an attached 20 ft. x 20 ft. garage. Suppose also that
- the land value is $200,000,
- the replacement cost of the house is $150 per square foot,
- the replacement cost of the garage is $40 per square foot,
- the estimated useful life of similar houses and garages is 50 years, and
- the effective age of this house and garage is 20 years.

Problem: What is the estimated value of the subject property?

Cost Approach Solution:

Subject value = land value + replacement cost - accrued depreciation.

Replacement cost of the house = 50 ft. x 40 ft. x $150/ ft.^{2} = $300,000
Replacement cost of the garage = 20 ft. x 20 ft. x $40/ ft.^{2} = $16,000
Total replacement cost = $300,000 + $16,000 = $316,000

Because the useful life is 50 years, using the straight-line method the rate of depreciation is 100% ÷ 50 years = 2% per year.
The effective age is 20 years, so the accrued depreciation percent in this case would be 20 years x 2% per year = 40%
40% of $316,000 = $126,400 = the accrued depreciation.

  $316,000 replacement cost
- $126,400 accrued depreciation
  $189,600 present value of the house and garage
+$200,000 land value
  $389,600 estimated of value of subject property

Example: The estimated cost to reproduce an office building with an estimated useful life of 40 years is $1,500,000. The land the building is on is valued at $750,000. Using the straight-line method of depreciation, what is the value of the property, assuming the actual age of the building is 12 years.

Answer: Annual depreciation = cost to reproduce ÷ useful life in years.
Annual depreciation = $1,500,000 ÷ 40 = $37,500.
Accrued depreciation = $37,500 × 12 = $450,000.
Property value = (reproduction cost - accrued depreciation) + land value.
Property value = ($1,500,000 - $450,000) + $750,000 = $1,800,000.

Example: A building depreciates by 2% each year. How many years will it take for the building to be worth only 80% of its initial value?

Answer: The answer can be rephrased as: How long does it take to depreciate by 20%. Since the building depreciates 2%/yr., it takes 20% ÷ 2%/yr. = 10 years.

Example: After owning a building for three years, Brian sold it for $1,455,000. His initial cost for the building was $1,500,000. What was the average annual rate of depreciation (loss in value) of the building?

Answer: Loss = $1,500,000 - $1,455,000 = $45,000.
Average annual loss = $45,000 ÷ 3 years = $15,000/yr.
$15,000/yr. ÷ $1,500,000 = 1% per year.

Income Approach

The *income approach* (also referred to as the *capitalization approach*) estimates the value of an income-producing property as being worth the present value of the future income of the property through a three-step process:

1. determine the net annual income,

2. determine an appropriate capitalization rate, and

3. divide the net income by the capitalization rate to obtain the estimate of value; i.e., value = net income ÷ capitalization rate.

Net operating income (NOI) is determined as follows:

a) estimate the potential annual gross income the property;

b) deduct from the gross income an annual allowance for vacancies and uncollectible rents to arrive at the *effective gross income*; and

c) deduct from the effective gross income the estimate of annual operating expenses, including fixed expenses (such as hazard insurance and real estate taxes), maintenance, and reserves for replacements of building components. (Note: *Not all expenses are deducted from effective gross income to obtain net income. Examples of such expenses include mortgage payments and taxes on income*)

Example: An apartment building produces an annual gross income of $2,500,000. Vacancies and uncollectible rents are running 8%. Monthly operating expenses are $135,400. What is the annual NOI?

Answer: Vacancies and uncollectible rents = $2,500,000 × .08 = $200,000.
Annual operating expenses = $135,400 × 12 = $1,624,800.
NOI = $2,500,000 - ($200,000 + $1,624,800) = $675,200.

The *capitalization rate* (also referred to as the *cap rate*) is the rate that an appraiser estimates is the yield rate expected by investors from comparable properties in current market conditions. To estimate the capitalization rate of a certain property, an appraiser will collect data on the market value of comparable properties, on the vacancies and uncollectible rents of these comparable properties, and on the operating expenses of these comparable properties. Then, because value = net income ÷ capitalization rate, the capitalization rate can be calculated for these comparable properties as net income ÷ market value.

Example: If the net annual income of a property is $20,000 and the capitalization rate is 8.5% per year, what would be the income approach valuation of the property?

Answer: $20,000 ÷ 8.5% = $235,294 (rounded).

Example: The above example might also take the following form: if an investor purchased a property for $235,294 and derives an annual net income from the property of $20,000, what is the property's capitalization rate?

Answer: $20,000 ÷ $235,294 = 8.5%.

Example of Income Approach

Assume that an apartment building has the following:

- 10 rental units each having fair market rent of $2,000 per month
- estimated loss for vacancies and uncollectible rents is 10%
- annual fixed expenses (property tax, insurance, etc.) are $30,000
- annual maintenance expense is $45,000
- annual reserve for replacements is $20,000
- the appraiser's capitalization rate is 8%

Problem: What is the value of the apartment building?

Solution

gross income ($2,000/unit x 10 units x 12 months)	$240,000
less vacancies & collection loss (10% of $240,000):	- $24,000
effective gross income :	$216,000
less annual expenses and replacement reserves:	- $95,000
net operating income:	$121,000

value = $121,000 ÷ 8% = $1,512,500

A finance concept closely related to the capitalization rate is ***return on investment (ROI)***, which is the investor's cash flow (net income minus financing charges) divided by the investor's *actual cash investment* (as distinct from the purchase price). *Note that the capitalization rate and the ROI would be the same if the investor had paid all cash for the property because in such a case there would be no finance charges and the initial investment would be equal to the sale price.*

Gross Rent and Gross Income Multipliers.

As we have seen, the income approach uses capitalization of *net* income to arrive at the valuation of a property. However, some investors, especially of single-family homes, use a simpler method of determining value that compares the sales price of the property to either its gross rent or to its gross income. The ***gross rent multiplier***

(GRM) is defined as the sales price divided by the gross *monthly* rent. The **gross income multiplier (GIM)** is defined as the sales price divided by the gross *annual* income.

Example: The sales price of a house is $500,000 and the monthly gross rent is $2,000. What is the gross rent multiplier?

Answer: $500,000 ÷ $2,000 = 250, so the sales price is 250 times the monthly rental; i.e., the gross rent multiplier is 250.

Example: Suppose now that other comparable homes in the area have a gross rent multiplier similar to the home in the prior example. Further, suppose that a comparable home in the area with a fair market value of $800,000 is to be rented. Using the gross rent multiplier approach what would be the appropriate rent for this $800,000 home?

Answer: Using the gross rent multiplier approach, we can determine the monthly rent for this subject property by dividing the value ($800,000) by the gross rent multiplier (250) to get a rent of $3,200 per month.

Example: A condo rents for $2,500 per month. If the condo cost $450,000, what is the annual gross rental income rate of this property?

Answer: $2,500/mo. × 12 mo./yr. = $30,000 gross rent per year. $30,000/yr. ÷ $450,000 = 6.67% gross rental income per year.

Example: An apartment building worth $450,000 earns 9% gross annual income. What is the monthly gross income from this investment?

Answer: $450,000 at 9%/yr. = $40,500/yr. $40,500/yr. ÷ 12 mo./yr. = $3,375 monthly gross income.

Example: An auto repair building rents for $16,500 per month. If the building cost $2.4 million, what is the annual gross rental income rate of this property?

Answer: $16,500/ mo. × 12 mo./yr. = $198,000 gross rent per year. $198,000/yr. ÷ $2,400,000 = 8.25% annual gross rental per year.

Example: Two partners who own a building that produces rent of $16,000 per month. One partner owns a 45% interest in the building. How much rental income from the building does this partner earn each year?

Answer: The annual rental income is $16,000/mo. × 12 mo./yr. = $192,000/yr. 45% of $192,000/yr. = $86,400/yr.

Example: The sales price of a condominium is $1,600,000 and the monthly rent is $8,000. What is the gross rent multiplier?

Answer: $1,600,000 ÷ $8,000 = 200.

Question 10-58: Nearby homes comparable to Marjorie's have an average monthly gross rent multiplier of 300. The fair market value of Marjorie's home is $1,650,000.

Using the gross rent multiplier approach, what monthly rent should Marjorie get for renting her home?

Answer: $1,650,000 ÷ 300 = $5,500.

Example: A building leased by a restaurant generates gross monthly rentals of $3,600. It also takes in $200 per month for parking fees. The fair market value of the property is $1,116,000. What is the monthly gross rent multiplier for this property?

Answer: To calculate gross rent multipliers, we do not consider income from any source other than rents. Therefore, in this case
gross monthly rent multiplier = $1,116,000 ÷ $3,600 = 310.

Lease Income

There are five major types of leases:

1. *Gross Lease*. Under a gross lease (also referred to as a ***fixed lease***), the tenant pays a fixed rental amount, and the landlord pays all of the operating expenses for the premises.

2. *Net Lease*. Under a net lease, the tenant pays a fixed rental amount plus some of the landlord's operating expenses (such as a percent of property taxes). A common variation on the net lease is the ***triple net lease***, under which the tenant pays a fixed rent plus the landlord's property taxes, hazard insurance, and all maintenance costs not specifically reserved for the landlord's maintenance (such as repairs to the roof).

3. *Variable Lease*. A ***variable lease*** is a lease that provides for periodic rent increases from an initial fixed rent. There are two basic types of variable leases: a ***graduated lease*** (or ***step-up lease***) and an ***index lease***. A graduated lease provides for predetermined rent increases, either as a fixed percentage each year or other time interval, or as a fixed dollar amount after certain time intervals. An index lease is a variable lease that provides for periodic increases in rent based on an economic index not in the control of the lesser or lessee, such as the Consumer Price Index.

4. *Percentage Lease*. Under a percentage lease, which is often used in shopping centers, the tenant typically pays a base rent amount plus a percentage of the gross receipts of the tenant's business. The percentage of gross charged is usually dependent on the percent markup used in the tenant's business. Thus, under a percentage lease the percentage of gross paid by a grocery store is likely to be much less than the percentage of gross paid by a parking lot.

5. *Ground Lease*. Under a ground lease, a tenant leases land and agrees to construct a building or to make other significant improvement on the land. At the end of the lease term, the improvement becomes the property of the landlord. These leases tend to be for long periods in order to make it

economically viable for the tenant to incur the large expense of the construction.

Example: A graduated lease on a 10,000 ft.² building provides for rent of $.85 per square foot per month for the first year, with a $.05 per square foot per month increase every three years, beginning at the end of the first year of the lease term. What is the yearly rent on this building during the fifth year of the lease term?

Answer: During the fifth year the rent is $.95 per square foot per month ($.85 for year one, $.90 for years two through four, $.95 for years five through seven, etc). 10,000 ft.² × $.95/ft.²/mo. × 12 mo./yr. = $114,000 per year.

Example: A graduated lease on a 10,000 square-foot building provides for rent of $.90 per square foot per month for the first year with a 3% increase in rent each year beginning at the end of the first year of the lease term. What is the yearly rent on this building during the second year of the lease term?

Answer: At the beginning of the second year, the rent increases by 3%. Therefore, during the second year of the lease term the rent is $.90 × 1.03 = $.927 per square foot per month. 10,000 ft.² × $.927/ft.²/mo. × 12 mo. = $111,240.

Example: A store in a mall has a percentage lease that provides for a fixed monthly rent of $2,500, plus 5% of gross sales. If gross sales average $12,750 per month during the year, what does the store pay for rent for the year?

Answer: The fixed annual rent is $2,500/mo. × 12 mo. = $30,000. The total gross sales are $12,750/mo. × 12 mo. = $153,000. Therefore, total rent for the year is $30,000 + ($153,000 × .05) = $37,650.

1031 Exchanges

A *1031 exchange* is a tax-deferred exchange (often misleadingly called a tax-free exchange) of "like kind" property held for productive use. In general, this means that any property held for business use or investment can be exchanged for any other like-kind property held for business use or investment (for example, a farm can be exchanged for an apartment building), though rules for exchanges of personal property (such as office furniture) are a bit more involved than are exchanges of real property. *A personal residence does not qualify for a 1031 exchange, nor do vacation or second homes, unless they are held as rentals for sufficient periods of time pursuant to IRS Rev Proc 2008-16.*

If a 1031 exchange has been properly structured, neither gain nor loss is recognized at the time of the exchange. If, on the other hand, a like-kind property is received in exchange along with *boot* (cash or other not like-kind property), gain is recognized on the value of the boot at the time of the exchange, but losses are still excluded from recognition at the time of the exchange.

Example: If an apartment building with a adjusted cost basis of $2 million is exchanged for an office building worth $2.3 million plus $100,000 cash (resulting in a $400,000 gain to the apartment building owner), what is the boot and when will it be recognized as taxable income?

Answer: The not like-kind amount in this example is the $100,000, and it will be recognized as taxable income at the time of the exchange.

Example: In the above example, when will the additional $300,000 in like-kind property the apartment owner received be recognized as taxable income?

Answer: The $300,000 additional gain the apartment owner received due to the greater value of the like-kind property received will not be recognized at the time of the exchange, but the cost basis of the $2.3 million office building will be lowered to $2 million, so that the additional $300,000 gain will be recognized when the newly acquired property is eventually sold.

Chapter 5 Quiz

Question: 1: A building depreciates by 3% per year. How many years will it take for the building to be worth only 70% of its initial value?

a. 10 years

b. 23⅓ years

c. 15 years

d. none of the above

Question 2: Amelia rents her home for $3,500 per month. If the house cost $750,000, what is the annual gross rental income rate of this property?

a. .00278%

b. .47%

c. 5.6%

d. 3.2%

Question 3: George owns an apartment building worth $6,500,000 on which he earns 8% gross annual income. What is his monthly gross income from this investment, rounded to the nearest dollar?

a. $43,333

b. $40,500

c. $405,000

d. $36,450

Question 4: After owning a building for four years, Marvin sold it for $1,536,000. His initial cost for the building was $1,600,000. What was the average annual rate of depreciation (loss in value) of the building (rounded to the nearest hundredth percent?

a. 1.00%

b. 2.08%

c. 1.04%

d. 2.86%

Question 5: The annual net operating income of an apartment building is $120,000. An appraiser estimated the value of the property at $1,500,000. What capitalization rate did the appraiser use to arrive at her valuation?

a. 16%

b. 8%

c. 4 %

d. none of the above

Question 6: A graduated lease on a 5,000 ft.² building provides for rent of $.80 per square foot per month for the first year, with a $.05 per square foot per month increase every three years, beginning at the end of the first year of the lease term. What is the yearly rent on this building during the third year of the lease term?

a. $4,250

b. $54,000

c. $51,000

d. $4,500

Question 7: Three similar properties in the area have fair market values and monthly rentals as follows: Comparable 1 — $267,540; $980. Comparable 2 — $274,560; $960. Comparable 3; $292,800; $960. What is the average gross rent multiplier for these properties?

a. 283

b. 284

c. 295

d. none of the above

Question 8: If the net monthly income of a property is $30,000 and the capitalization rate is 7.5% per year, what would be the income approach valuation of the property?

a. $200,000

b. $400,000

c. $250,000

d. $4,800,000

Question 9: A small office building generates gross monthly rentals of $4,400. It also takes in $250 per month for parking fees. The fair market value of the property is $1,232,000. What is the gross rent multiplier for this property?

a. 265 (rounded)

b. 273 (rounded)

c. 294 (rounded)

d. none of the above

Question 10: A graduated lease on a 7,500 square-foot building provides for rent of $.80 per square foot per month for the first year with a 2% increase in rent each year beginning at the end of the first year of the lease term. What is the yearly rent on this building during the second year of the lease term?

a. $6,120

b. $73,440

c. $6,240

d. $74,880

Question 11: The subject property and a comparable are homes except that the comparable as an inferior guesthouse estimated to be worth $3,500 less than the subject guesthouse, and the comparable has superior landscaping estimated to be worth $1,000 more than the subject landscaping. What adjustments should be made?

a. The comparable value should be adjusted down by $2,500

b. The comparable value should be adjusted up by $2,500.

c. The subject value should be adjusted down by $2,500.

d. The subject value should be adjusted up by $2,500.

Question 12: Susan and Janet are partners who own a building that produces rent of $18,000 per month. Janet owns a 48% interest in the building. How much rental income from the building does Susan earn each year?

a. $103,680

b. $450,000

c. $8,500

d. none of the above

Question 13: The sales price of a single-family home is $480,000 and the monthly rent is $1,600. What is the gross rent multiplier?

a. 200

b. 150

c. 300

d. none of the above

Question 14: Arnold sold a vacant lot for $2,250,125 that he had purchased 5 years earlier for $2,350,000. What was the average annual rate of loss in value of the lot?

a. .85%

b. .89%

c. 4.44%

d. none of the above

Question 15: A gas station has a percentage lease that provides for a fixed monthly rent of $15,000, plus 2% of gross sales. If gross sales average $200,000 per month during the year, what does the gas station pay for rent for the year?

a. $228,000

b. $240,000

c. $184,000

d. $48,000

Question 16: A building depreciates by 4% each year. How many years will it take for the building to be worth only 40% of its initial value?

a. 10 years

b. 18 years

c. 16 years

d. none of the above

Question 17: A single-family home rents for $10,500 per month. If the house cost $2 million, what is the annual gross rental income rate of this property?

a. 6.3%

b. 5.25 %

c. 0.525 %

d. 8.33%

Question 18: A property comparable to a subject property as an inferior pool estimated to be worth $2,500 less than the subject pool, and the comparable has superior landscaping estimated to be worth $3,500 more than the subject landscaping. What adjustments should be made?

a. adjust the subject property value up by $1,000

b. adjust the subject property value down by $1,000

c. adjust the comparable property value up by $1,000

d. adjust the comparable property value down by $1,000

Question 19: What is the value of a property based on the following information?
Estimated annual gross income: $85,000
Vacancies and uncollectible rents: 7%
Annual maintenance expenses and utilities: $10,000
Annual property taxes: $9,500
Annual insurances: $1,500
Monthly mortgage payment: $2,500
Capitalization rate: 9.5%

a. $626,842 (rounded)

b. $611,053 (rounded)

c. $778,947 (rounded)

d. none of the above

Question 20: The monthly net operating income of Sherry's property is $45,000 and the capitalization rate is 6.5% per year. What is the value of Sherry's property based on an income valuation of the property, rounded to the nearest dollar?

a. $1,351,000

b. $692,308

c. $500,000

d. $8,307,692

Question 21: An office building produces an annual gross income of $3,950,000. Vacancies and uncollectible rents are running 8%. Monthly operating expenses are $245,400. What is the annual NOI?

a. $3,388,600

b. $689,200

c. $1,982,400

d. none of the above

Question 22: The monthly net operating income of a property is $85,000 and the capitalization rate is 5.5% per year, what would be the value of the property based on an income valuation of the property, rounded to the nearest dollar?

a. $1,545,455

b. $933,334

c. $18,545,455

d. none of the above

Question 23: The estimated cost to reproduce an apartment building with an estimated useful life of 50 years is $3,500,000. The land the building is on is valued at $750,000. Using the straight-line method of depreciation, what is the value of the property, assuming the actual age of the building is 12 years.

a. $2,660,000

b. $4,180,000

c. $2,437,500

d. $3,410,000

Question 24: Homes comparable to Alan's in the area have an average gross rent multiplier of 290. The fair market value of Alan's home is $1,841,500. Using the gross rent multiplier approach, what monthly rent should Alan get for renting her home?

a. $6,350

b. $8,715

c. $6,214 (rounded)

d. none of the above

Question 25: Margaret purchases an apartment building for $3,000,000 that has a useful life of 40 years and an anticipated residual value of $850,000. After 10 years, what is the value of the building, if by "value" we mean the original cost less accumulated straight-line depreciation?

a. $2,462,500

b. $2,250,000

c. $2,150,000

d. $2,037,500

Chapter 5 Quiz Answers

Answer 1: **a.** It takes $30 \div 3 = 10$ years to depreciate by 30%, leaving 70% value.

Answer 2: **c.** \$3,500/mo. × 12 mo./yr. = \$42,000 rent per year.
\$42,000/yr. ÷ \$750,000 = 5.6% per year.

Answer 3: **a.** \$6,500,000 at 8%/yr. = \$520,000/yr.
\$520,000/yr. ÷ 12 mo./yr. = \$43,333/mo. (rounded)

Answer 4: **a.** Loss = \$1,600,000 - \$1,536,000 = \$64,000.
Average annual loss = \$64,000 ÷ 4 years = \$16,000/yr.
\$16,000/yr. ÷ \$1,600,000 = 1% per year.

Answer 5: **b.** \$120,000 ÷ \$1,500,000 = 8%.

Answer 6: **c.** During the third year the rent is \$.85 per square foot per month (\$.80 for year one, \$.85 for years two through four, \$.90 for years five through seven, etc).
5,000 ft.² × \$.85/ft.²/mo. × 12 mo./yr. = \$51,000 per year.

Answer 7: **a.** Comparable 1: \$267,540 ÷ \$980 = 273.
Comparable 2: \$274,560 ÷ \$960 = 286.
Comparable 3: \$292,800 ÷ \$960 = 305.
(273 + 286 + 305) ÷ 3 = 288.

Answer 8: **d.** (\$30,000 × 12) ÷ 7.5% = \$4,800,000.

Answer 9: **d.** To calculate gross rent multipliers, we do not consider income from any source other than rents. Therefore, in this case
gross monthly rent multiplier = \$1,232,000 ÷ \$4,400 = 280.

Answer 10: **b.** At the beginning of the second year, the rent increases by 2%. Therefore, during the second year of the lease term the rent is \$.80 × 1.02 = \$.816 per square foot per month. 7,500 ft.² × \$.816/ft.²/mo. × 12 mo. = \$73,440.

Answer 11: **b.** The comparable has a guesthouse and landscaping combined value of \$2,500 *less* than the subject view and landscaping value. Therefore, the comparable value should be *adjusted up* by \$2,500.

Answer 12: **d.** The annual rental income is \$18,000/mo. x 12 mo./yr. = \$216,000/yr. *Susan's* interest is 52%, therefore, her annual rental income from the building is 52% of \$216,000/yr. = \$112,320/yr.

Answer 13: **c.** \$480,000 ÷ \$1,600 = 300.

Answer 14: **a.** Loss = \$2,350,000 - \$2,250,125 = \$99,875.
Average annual loss = \$99,875 ÷ 5 years = \$19,975/yr.
\$19,975/yr. ÷ \$2,350,000 = .85% per year.

Answer 15: **a.** The fixed annual rent is \$15,000/mo. × 12 mo. = \$180,000. The total gross sales are \$200,000/mo. × 12 mo. = \$2,400,000. Therefore, total rent for the

year is
$180,000 + ($2,400,000 \times .02) = $228,000.

Answer 16: **d.** The answer can be rephrased as: How long does it take to depreciate by 60%. Since the building depreciates 4%/yr., it takes 60% ÷ 4%/yr. = 15 years.

Answer 17: **a.** $10,500/ mo. × 12 mo./yr. = $126,000 rent per year. $126,000/yr. ÷ $2,000,000 = 6.3% per year.

Answer 18: **d.** The comparable has a pool and landscaping combined value of $1,000 more than the subject pool and landscaping value. Therefore, the comparable value should be adjusted down by $1,000.

Answer 19: **b.** $85,000 × .07 = $5,950 (vacancy and uncollectible rents losses). $85,000 - $5,950 = $79,050 (effective gross income). $79,050 - $21,000 (operating expenses) = $58,050 (NOI). *Note that monthly mortgage payments are disregarded when calculating net operating income.* $58,050 ÷ .095 = $611,053 (rounded).

Answer 20: **d.** Because the *monthly* net operating income is $35,000, the annual net operating income is $45,000 × 12 = $540,000. $540,000 ÷ 6.5% = $8,307,692 (rounded).

Answer 21: **b.** $3,950,000 × .08 = $316,000. Annual operating expenses = $245,400 × 12 = $2,944,800. NOI = $3,950,000 − ($316,000 + $2,944,800) = $689,200.

Answer 22: **c.** ($85,000 × 12) ÷ 5.5% = $1,545,455 (rounded).

Answer 23: **d.** Annual depreciation = cost to reproduce ÷ useful life in years. Annual depreciation = $3,500,000 ÷ 50 = $70,000. Accrued depreciation = $70,000 × 12 = $840,000. Property value = (reproduction cost - accrued depreciation) + land value. Property value = ($3,500,000 - $840,000) + $750,000 = $3,410,000.

Answer 24: **a.** $1,841,500 ÷ 290 = $6,350.

Answer 25: **a.** Annual depreciation = (cost of property - residual value) ÷ useful life of property. Therefore, annual depreciation = ($3,000,000 - $850,000) ÷ 40 = $53,750. Accumulated straight-line depreciation equals $53,750 × 10 = $537,500. $3,000,000 - $537,500 = $2,462,500.

CHAPTER 6: PRORATION AT CLOSING

When calculating proration problems, it is important to know what ***day count convention*** to use. An exact calculation would take into account the precise number of days: 30 days for some months, 31 or 28 or 29 for other months; 365 days for some years, 366 for leap years. In the days before computers, such calculations would have been quite burdensome, so the ***30/360 day count convention*** was adopted to simplify certain calculations. When using the 30/360 day count convention, each month is considered to have 30 days, and each year is considered to have 360 days. A year consisting of 360 days with 12 months of 30 days each is often referred to as a ***statutory year***, or a ***banker's year***. The 30/360 day count convention for calculating *proration, interest, insurance premiums*, and similar expenses is standard in the real estate market. However, in some areas, rules for calculating proration, interest, etc., are based on the actual number of days in a month or year.

Proration questions that appear on your real estate exam will state whether calculations should be based on a 30-day month, on a 360- or 365-day year, and whether the day of closing belongs to the seller or to the buyer.

As a general rule, at the close of escrow in a real estate transaction, certain allocations of expenses incurred in the ordinary course of property ownership must be made. For example, if the escrow closes midyear or midmonth, the seller may have prepaid taxes, insurance, or association dues, in which case credit to the seller's account should be made. Conversely, if the seller is behind on paying taxes or insurance, etc., the seller's account should be debited. Such an adjustment of expenses that either have been paid or are in arrears in proportion to actual time of ownership as of the closing or other agreed-upon date is called ***proration***. Proration, like ordinary interest, is generally calculated according to the 30/360 day count convention (statutory year).

To compute proration, follow these steps:

1. determine which, if any, expenses are to be prorated;
2. determine to whom the expenses should be credited or debited;
3. determine how many days the expenses are to be prorated;
4. calculate the per day proration amount; and
5. multiply the number of days by the per day proration amount.

Proration of Rent

Example: Buyer purchases from Seller a condo that rents for $2,400 a month, with rent due on the first of each month for that month's rent. Escrow closes on June 16. Who pays whom how much in regard to proration of the rent?

Answer: Because rent was paid in advance, Seller should credit Buyer for 15 days rent, which is $1,200.

Example: Susan purchased a condo for $200,000 that Bob had rented to Joe at $1,500 a month. Escrow closed on September 16. How should the $200,000 selling price be adjusted at close of escrow if the day of closing belongs to the buyer?

Answer: Rent is normally collected *in advance* on the first day of the month, so unless stated otherwise one should make this assumption in proration of rent problems. Under this assumption, Bob received $1,500 on or about September 1, but only deserved to keep half of the month's rent because Susan acquired ownership of the condo on September 16. Therefore, Susan should be credited $750 at the close of escrow.

Example: Referring to the above example, suppose that escrow closed on October 16 rather than on September 16. Because October has 31 days, we would need to know whether the calculation should be based on calendar months or on the 30-day convention. If the problem stated that calendar months should be used for the calculation, how should the $200,000 selling price be adjusted at close of escrow?

Answer: Because October has 31 days and we are using a calendar month for our calculation, the per diem rental amount is $1,500 \div 31 = 48.387, rounded to the nearest 10th of a cent. We are told that October 16 belongs to the buyer, Susan, so Susan should be credited for 31-15 = 16 days. $16 \times $48.387 = 774.19, rounded to the nearest cent.

Proration of Mortgage Payments

Example: Kathy purchased a home from Martin on which Martin had an outstanding loan balance of $245,000 on November 20, the day that escrow closed. The interest rate on the loan was 6% and was payable in arrears with the loan payment on the first of each month. If Kathy assumed Martin's loan, who should have paid whom in regard to proration of the interest and by how much if the day of closing belongs to the buyer, and calculations are based on a statutory year?

Answer: The seller, Martin, owned the home for 19 days before closing — 19 days for which he had not paid the interest on the loan as of the closing of escrow. Kathy should, therefore, have been credited for 19 day's interest.

The annual interest on the loan was 6%, and $245,000 was the loan balance on which interest would be paid by Kathy on December 1. Figured on an *annual* basis, interest of 6% on $245,000 = $14,700, so to obtain the *daily* interest amount for each day of April we divide $14,700 by 360 (using a statutory year) to get $40.8333. [Note that in proration problems it is best to use at least four numbers after the decimal point until you get to the final answer, which can be rounded off.] Because Kathy should have been credited for 19 days, her credit should have been 19 × $40.8333= $775.83.

Proration of Homeowner's Fees

Example: John sold his condo to Gordon, closing date July 16. John had prepaid his monthly homeowner's fee of $527 on the first of the month. How much of the homeowner's fee must the buyer reimburse John for if a calendar year is used for the calculation and the closing day belongs to the buyer?

Answer: The number of days the buyer must reimburse John for is 31-15 = 16. The daily rate of the homeowner's fee for October was $527 ÷ 31 = $17. Therefore the buyer must reimburse John in an amount of $17 × 16 = $272.

Proration of Taxes

Example: Janet sells her condo to Martha for $200,000, closing date May 16. If property taxes on the condo are $1,800 for each six-months, payable in arrears on July 1 and January 1 of each year, and if proration is calculated on the basis of a banker's year (statutory year), what is the proration amount at closing and is who credited/debited if the day of closing belongs to the buyer?

Answer: Using the banker's year of 30 days per month, at the closing Janet is in arrears in her payment of taxes by 15 days in May, and by 4 × 30 = 120 days for January through April, total 135 days. Because there are 180 days in six months of a banker's year, the per day tax rate on the $1,800 tax bill is $10. Therefore, 135 days × $10 per day = $1,350, which should be debited to Janet and credited to the Martha.

Chapter 6 Quiz

Question: 1. Buyer purchases from Seller a condo that rents for $2,450 a month, with rent due on the first of each month for that month's rent. Escrow closes on June 16. Who pays whom how much in regard to proration of the rent?

a. Buyer should credit Seller $1,225

b. Seller should credit Buyer $1,225

c. Buyer should credit Seller $2,450

d. Seller should credit Buyer $2,450

Question 2: Gordon sold his condo to Sandra, closing date March 7. Gordon had prepaid his monthly homeowner's fee of $465 on the first of the month. How much of the homeowner's fee must the buyer reimburse Gordon for if a calendar year is used for the calculation and the closing day belongs to the buyer?

a. $360

b. $375

c. $225

d. none of the above

Question 3: Amelia sells her condo to Kathy for $100,000, closing date June 16. If property taxes on the condo are $900 for each six-months, payable in arrears on July 1 and January 1 of each year, and if proration is calculated on the basis of a banker's year (statutory year), what is the proration amount at closing and is who credited/debited if the day of closing belongs to the buyer?

a. $450 debited to Kathy

b. $825 debited to Kathy

c. $825 debited to Amelia

d. none of the above

Question 4: Betty purchased a condo from Dave on which Dave had an outstanding loan balance of $275,000 on June 20, the day that escrow closed. The interest rate on the loan was 4% and was payable with the loan payment in arrears on the first of each month. If Betty assumed Dave's loan, who should have paid whom in regard to proration of the interest and by how much, rounded to the nearest cent, if the day of closing belongs to the buyer and calculations are based on a statutory year?

a. Betty should have been credited $580.56.

b. Dave should have been credited $580.56.

c. Neither Dave nor Betty should have credited the other anything.

d. None of the above.

Question 5: Buyer purchased a condo for $175,000 that had been rented from Seller at $1,705 a month, with rent payable in advance on the first of each month. Escrow closed on July 21. How should the $175,000 selling price be adjusted at close of escrow, rounded to the nearest dollar, if the day of closing belongs to the buyer and calculations are based on a calendar year?

a. Buyer must credit Seller for $568.

b. Buyer must credit Seller for $550.

c. Seller must credit Buyer for $605.

d. None of the above.

Chapter 6 Quiz Answers

Answer 1: **b.** Because rent is paid in advance, Seller should credit Buyer for 15 days rent, which is $2,450 × ½ = $1,225.

Answer 2: **b.** The number of days the buyer must reimburse Gordon for is 31- 6 = 25. The daily rate of the homeowner's fee for October was $465 ÷ 31 = $15. Therefore the buyer must reimburse Bob in an amount of $15 × 25 = $375.

Answer 3: **c.** Using the banker's year of 30 days per month, at the closing Amelia is in arrears in her payment of taxes by 15 days in June, and by 5 × 30 = 150 days for January through May, total 165 days. Because there are 180 days in six months of a banker's year, the per day tax rate on the $900 tax bill is $5. Therefore, 165 days × $5 per day = $825, which should be debited to Amelia and credited to the Kathy.

Answer 4: **a.** The seller, Dave, owned the condo for 19 days before closing — 19 days for which he had not paid the interest on the loan as of the closing of escrow. Betty should, therefore, have been credited for 19 day's interest.

The annual interest on the loan was 4%, and $275,000 was the loan balance on which interest would be paid by Betty (who assumed the loan) on July 1. Figured on an *annual* basis, interest of 4% on $275,000 = $11,000, so to obtain the *daily* interest amount for each day of April we divide $11,000 by 360 (using a statutory year) to get $30.5556. [Note that in proration problems it is best to use at least four numbers after the decimal point until you get to the final answer, which can be rounded off.] Because Betty should have been credited for 19 days, her credit should have been 19 × $30.5556= $580.56, rounded to the nearest cent.

Answer 5: **c.** Calculations are to be made using a calendar year. Therefore, we must consider July as having 31 days. The per diem rent is $1,705 ÷ 31 = $55. Because closing day belongs to Buyer, Seller must credit Buyer for 31 – 20 = 11 days at $55 per day = $605.

PRACTICE EXAM 1

1.   Robert sold a house for $415,000 and received $10,375 in commission from his broker. What commission rate did Robert receive on the sale?

a. 3%

b. 3.5%

c. 2.5%

d. 2%

2.   A triangular lot with a height 125 feet and a base of 85 feet sold for $12 per square foot. What did the lot sell for?

a. $119,700

b. $60,000

c. $127,500

d. $63,750

3.   A 15,000 ft.² lot costs $21 per square foot. The 2,700 ft.² house on the lot costs $125 per square foot, and the 430 ft.² garage costs $35 per square foot. How much does this property cost?

a. $652,550

b. $667,550

c. $654,050

d. none of the above

4.   Nelson's lender required a 15% down payment to obtain the mortgage on his house. The down payment amount was $67,500. What was the purchase price that Nelson paid for his house?

a. $79,412 (rounded to the nearest dollar)

b. $101,250

c. $450,000

d. $382,500

5.   Betty is purchasing a house for $350,000 with 20% down and has negotiated a very favorable interest rate. However, in order to obtain this favorable interest rate, the lender requires that Betty pay 1.5 discount points upfront. How much will Betty pay the lender for these discount points?

a. $4,200

b. $2,800

c. $280

d. $420

6.   Carla purchased a home for $200,000 with a 4 % fixed-rate, fully amortized 30-year loan in the principal amount of $170,010. She makes payments of $850 per month. What is the amount of unpaid principal on this loan after the first month's payment?

a. $169,726.70

b. $169,826.67

c. $168,593.30

d. none of the above

7.   A warehouse is 22 yards wide, 23 yards long, and 32 feet high. How many cubic feet are contained in this warehouse?

a. 16,192 ft.^{3}

b. 145,728 ft.^{3}

c. 437,184 ft.^{3}

d. 48,576 ft.^{3}

8.   Margaret procured a listing and a sale for a condo with list price of $175,000. The seller agreed to pay Margaret's broker a commission of 5% of the sales price. Margaret's agreement with her broker is that she would receive 50% of any commission received by her broker coming from sales that she procures. With the help of a cooperating broker — who had a commission split agreement with Margaret's employing broker whereby Margaret's employing broker would receive 60% and the cooperating broker would receive 40% of the commission — the house eventually sold for 90% of the list price. What was Margaret's commission on this transaction?

a. $2,362.50

b. $1968.75

c. $2,590.75

d. $2,625

9.   Nelson sold his condo for $222,000 six years after he purchased it for $180,000. At what annual rate did Nelson profit from his investment?

a. 2.2% (rounded)

b. 3.2 % (rounded)

c. 3.9 % (rounded)

d. 3.1 % (rounded)

10.   Larry's lender is willing to loan 85% of the lesser of the purchase price of his house and the appraised value of the house. The purchase price of the house is $340,000. The loan amount is $275,000. What is the appraised value of the house, rounded to the nearest dollar?

a. $289,000

b. $323,529

c. $210,000

d. $195,000

11.   A lender requires a yield on a loan that is .9% greater than the quoted interest rate on the loan. How many discount points must this lender charge the borrower in order to obtain the lender's required yield if to reduce the interest rate by .15% the lender must charge one discount point?

a. 3 discount points

b. 5 discount points

c. 6 discount points

d. 4 discount points

12.   The cost of a 35,000 square-foot lot is $30,800. What is the cost per square foot?

a. $1.14 (rounded)

b. $.86 (rounded)

c. $.75

d. none of the above

13.   Eva received a loan with an LTV of 80% to purchase a home that had a sales price of $275,000 and an appraised value of $280,000. What is the amount of Eva's loan if the LTV was based on the lesser of the appraised value or the sales price?

a. $220,000

b. $224,000

c. $222,000

d. none of the above

14.   Anita is purchasing a house for $375,000 with 10% down. The lender requires 4.5 discount points. How much will Anita pay the lender for the discount points?

a. $13,500

b. $12,000

c. $15,187.50

d. $13,000

15.   Gary has just arranged to obtain a home equity line of credit of 80% of the appraised value of his home, minus the total indebtedness against his home. The appraised value of his home is $200,000. The line of credit is $60,000. What is the total indebtedness against Gary's home?

a. $80,000

b. $100,000

c. $175,000

d. None of the above

16.   The selling price of the home Lisa is purchasing $275,000. The lender is willing to loan 80% of the lesser of the purchase price or the appraised value. If the amount the lender is willing to loan is $220,000, what is the appraised value of Lisa's home?

a. $270,000

b. $250,000

c. $265,000

d. none of the above

17.   A home has a fair market value of $550,000, a homestead exemption of $100,000, an assessed value of $468,000, a county property tax of 1.2%, and a city property tax of .75%. What is the annual property tax on this home?

a. $8,775

b. $7,176

c. $7,360

d. none of the above

18.   Joe is a resident manager who receives a 3% commission on rents from an apartment building that he manages. If Joe leases Susan an apartment for three years with rents starting at $750 per month for the first year and increasing by $50 per month for each succeeding year, and if Susan remains in possession of the apartment for the full three years, how much commission will Joe receive from Susan's lease?

a. $864

b. $810

c. $216

d. none of the above

19.   Sophie is a real estate salesperson who procured a buyer for a home. Sophie's agreement with her employing broker, Eva, is that Sophie gets a commission of 40% of whatever commission that Eva receives on sales made by Sophie. Sophie procures

a sale of a house that was listed by John, who had an 50-50 commission-split agreement with Eva. Sophie's commission on the sale was $4,074. The listing agreement provided for a 6% commission. What was the sales price of the house?

a. $271,600

b. $339,500

c. $424,375

d. none of the above

20.   Ernesto sold his house, receiving $423,000 after paying a 6% commission. For how much did Ernesto sell his house?

a. $400,000

b. $423,000

c. $475,000

d. none of the above

21.   Emily purchased a home from Bob on which Bob had an outstanding loan balance of $385,000 on April 20, the day that escrow closed. The interest rate on the loan was 5% and was payable with the loan payment on the first of each month. If Emily assumed Bob's loan, who should have paid whom in regard to proration of the interest and by how much if the interest on the loan is due after it has accrued, the day of closing belongs to the buyer, and calculations are based on a statutory year?

a. Emily should have been paid $1,015.97

b. Bob should have been paid $1,015.97

c. neither Bob nor Emily should have paid the other anything

d. none of the above

22.   The subject property and a comparable are homes that appear almost exactly the same except that the comparable as an inferior pool estimated to be worth $2,000 less than the subject pool, and the comparable has superior landscaping estimated to be worth $1,500 more than the subject landscaping. What adjustments should be made?

a. adjust the subject property value up by $500

b. adjust the subject property value down by $500

c. adjust the comparable property value up by $500

d. adjust the comparable property value down by $500

23.   The estimated cost to reproduce an office building with an estimated useful life of 40 years is $2,500,000. The land the building is on is valued at $850,000.

Using the straight-line method of depreciation, what is the value of the property, assuming the actual age of the building is 12 years.

a. $1,750,000

b. $1,650,000

c. $2,437,500

d. none of the above

24.   Using the gross rent multiplier approach, suppose the sales price of a condominium is $2,700,000 and the monthly rent is $9,000. What is the gross rent multiplier?

a. 200

b. 150

c. 300

d. none of the above

25.   Bob owns a three-acre rectangular lot and wishes to divide it into 5 lots, each having a depth of 70 yards. What would be the width of each of these lots?

a. 41.49 feet

b. 207.43 feet

c. 124.46 feet

d. 622.29 feet

26.   Jessica wants to deposit enough money into a savings account that pays 1.5% annual interest to earn $500 each month. How much would Jessica have to deposit earn this much?

a. $33,333.33

b. $400,000

c. $333,333.33

d. none of the above

27.   Julie is a salesperson who receives 40% of the commission on all sales that her employing broker, Susan, receives due to Julie's effort. Julie receives a commission of $9,350 due to her procurement of the sale of a house for which Susan had a 5% commission listing agreement. How much did the house sell for?

a. $187,000

b. $467,500

c. $233,750

d. $311,667

28. Joe owns a 3-acre rectangular lot that he wants to divide into 5 lots of equal size, each having a depth of 150 feet. What would be the width of each of these lots?

a. 174.24 feet

b. 290.40 feet

c. 170.24 feet

d. none of the above

29. Carla makes payments of $850 per month, including 4% interest on a fixed-rate, fully amortized 30-year loan. What was the initial amount of her loan, rounded to the nearest dollar?

Monthly Payment Per $1,000 on Fixed-Rate, Fully Amortized Loans				
Rate	10-year term	15-year term	30-year term	40-year term
4%	10.125	7.397	4.775	4.180
5%	10.607	7.908	5.369	4.822
6%	11.102	8.439	5.996	5.503
7%	11.611	8.989	6.653	6.215
8%	12.133	9.557	7.338	6.954

a. $203,349

b. $170,010

c. $158,316

d. none of the above

30. What is the rectangular survey system legal description of the shaded area of Section 7 in the diagram below?

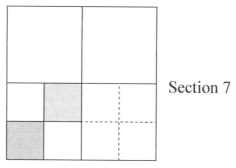 Section 7

a. SE¼ of the NE½ Section 7 and the NW¼ of the SE¼ of Section 7

b. NE¼ of the SE¼ of Section 7 and the N½ of the SW¼ of Section 7

c. NE¼ of the SE¼ of Section 7 and the SE¼ of the NE¼ of Section 7

d. SW¼ of the SW¼ of Section 7and the NE¼ of the SW¼ of Section 7

Practice Exam 1 Answers

1. Answer 4: c. $10,375 ÷ $415,000 = .025, which means that Robert received a commission rate of 2.5%.

2. Answer 8:   **d.** The area of the triangular lot is ½ (125 ft. × 85 ft.) = 5,312.5 ft.² Therefore, at a cost of $12/ ft.², the lot sold for 5,312.5 ft.² × $12/ft.² = $63,750.

3. Answer 12:   **b.** Lot: 15,000 ft.² x $21/ft.² = $315,000
House: 2,700 ft.² x 125/ft.² = $337,500
Garage: 430 ft.² x 35/ft.² = $15,050
Total = $667,550

4. Answer 16:   **c.** 15% of the purchase price = .15 × (purchase price) = $67,500. Dividing both sides of the equation by .15, we get purchase price = $450,000.

5. Answer 20:   **a.** Betty is putting 20% of $350,000 = $70,000 down. Therefore, the loan amount is $350,000 - $70,000 = $280,000. The cost to Betty of the discount points would therefore be $280,000 × .015 = $4,200.

6. Answer 88: a. $170,010 × .04 ÷ 12 = $566.70 (first month's interest)
$850 - $566.70 = $283.30 (first month's principal payment)
$170,010 - $283.30 = $169,726.70 (principal balance after first month's payment).

7. Answer 28:   **b.** The first thing we must do to perform calculations on problems that contain mixed units of measure to convert all measurements to the same dimension. Because the question asks for how many cubic feet, it makes sense to convert yards into feet. Doing this, the volume of this warehouse is
(22 yd. × 3 ft./yd.) × (23 yd. × 3 ft./yd.) × 32 ft. = 145,728 ft.³

8. Answer 32:   **a.** The house sold for 90% of $175,000 = .90 × $175,000 = $157,500. Therefore, the commission paid by the seller = 0.05 × $157,500 = $7,875. Margaret's employing broker received 60% of this commission = 0.6 × $7,875 = $4,725. Margaret received 50% of the commission received by her broker, which is 0.5 × $4,725 = $2,362.50.

9. Answer 36:   **c.** Nelson's profit on his condo was $222,000 - $180,000 = $42,000. Because this $42,000 profit was spread over six years, Nelson's annual profit was
$42,000 ÷ 6 = $7,000. Therefore, the annual rate of profit was
$7,000 ÷ $180,000 = .039 = 3.9% (rounded).

10. Answer 40:   **b.** Because 85% of the purchase price ($340,000) = $289,000, but the loan amount was only $275,000, we know that the appraised value of the house was less than the purchase price. In fact, we know that
85% of the appraised value of the house = $275,000. Therefore,
the appraised value of the house = $275,000 ÷ .85 = $323,529 (rounded).

11. Answer 44:   **c.** Since charging one discount point will raise the effective yield by .15%, the number of discount points needed are .9% ÷ .15% = 6 discount points.

12. Answer 48:   **d.** 35,000 ft.² × (cost per square foot) = $30,800. Cost per square foot = $30,800 ÷ 35,000 ft.² = $.88 per square foot.

13. Answer 52: a. Here, LTV = .80 = (amount of the loan) ÷ $275,000. Therefore, the amount of the loan is $275,000 × .80 = $220,000.

14. Answer 56: c. The loan amount is $375,000 - $37,500 (the down payment) = $337,500.
$337,500 × .045 = $15,187.50.

15. Answer 60: b. ($200,000 × .8) - (total indebtedness against the home) = $60,000.
$160,000 - (total indebtedness against the home) = $60,000.
Total indebtedness against the home = $100,000.

16. Answer 64: d. (the lesser of the appraised value or $275,000) × .8 = $220,000.
(the lesser of the appraised value or $275,000) = $220,000 ÷ .8 = $275,000.
Therefore, the appraised value of the home is $275,000 or greater.

17. Answer 68: b. ($468,000 - $100,000) × (.012 + .0075) = $7,176.

18. Answer 72: a. $750 × 12 months = $9,000. $800 × 12 months = $9,600. $850 × 12 months = $10,200. Total for the three years his $28,800. $28,800 × 3% = $864 commission.

19. Answer 76: b. Sophie's commission is 40% of 50% of 6% = 1.2% of the sales price. Therefore,
$4,074 = .012 × (sales price), so sales price = $339,500.

20. Answer 80: d. We are told that the price the house sold for minus the commission paid was $423,000. Therefore,
Sales Price - Commission = $423,000
Sales Price - (6% of Sales Price) = $423,000
Sales price - (.06 × Sales Price) = $423,000
.94 × Sales Price = $423,000
Finally, dividing both sides of the equation by .94, we get Sales Price = $450,000.

21. Answer 84: a. The seller, Bob, owned the home for 19 days before closing — 19 days for which he had not paid the interest on the loan as of the closing of escrow. Emily should, therefore, have been credited for 19 day's interest.

The annual interest on the loan was 5%, and $385,000 was the loan balance on which interest would be paid by Emily (who assumed the loan) on May 1. Figured on an *annual* basis, interest of 5% on $385,000 = $19,250, so to obtain the *daily* interest amount for each day of April we divide $19,250 by 360 (using a statutory year) to get $53.4722. [Note that in proration problems it is best to use at least four numbers after the decimal point until you get to the final answer, which can be rounded off.]

Because Emily should have been credited for 19 days, her credit should have been 19 × $53.4722 = $1,015.97.

22. Answer 92: c. The comparable has a pool and landscaping combined value of $500 less than the subject pool and landscaping value. Therefore, the comparable value should be adjusted up by $500.

23. Answer 96: d. Annual depreciation = cost to reproduce ÷ useful life in years.
Annual depreciation = $2,500,000 ÷ 40 = $62,500.
Accrued depreciation = $62,500 × 12 = $750,000.
Property value = (reproduction cost - accrued depreciation) + land value.
Property value = ($2,500,000 - $750,000) + $850,000 = $2,600,000.

24. Answer 100: c. $2,700,000 ÷ $9,000 = 300.

25. Answer 104: c. 3 x 43,560 ft.^{2} = 130,680 ft.^{2} as the area for the entire lot.
130,680 ft.^{2} ÷ 5 = 26,136 ft.^{2} per parcel.
26,136 ft.^{2} ÷ 210 ft. = 124.46 ft. width for each of the 5 parcels.

26. Answer 108: b. Jessica wants to earn the rate of $6,000 per year.
$6,000 ÷ 1.5% = $400,000.

27. Answer 112: b. Julie effectively receives 2% of the sales she makes from Susan's listing. Therefore, $9,350 = 2% of Sales Price. $9,350 ÷ .02 = $467,500.

28. Answer 116: a. Joe's 3-acre lot has 3 x 43,560 ft.^{2} = 130,680 ft.^{2}. Therefore, each of the equal-sized lots would be 130,680 ft.^{2} ÷ 5 = 26,136 ft.^{2}. 26,136 ft.^{2} ÷ 150 feet = 174.24 feet width.

29. Answer 120: d. Finding where 4% and a 30-year term intersect in the table, we obtain the number 4.775 which is the dollar amount per month per $1,000 of the initial loan.
$4.775/$1,000 = $850/loan amount. Therefore,
loan amount = ($850 ÷ $4.775) × $1,000 = $178,010 (rounded).

30. Answer 24. **d.** Because the shaded area extends into two distinct quarters of the section, we need to analyze each of the separate shaded areas separately. The area on the left is in the SW¼ of Section 7, and is in the SW¼ of the SW¼ of Section 7. The area on the upper right is in the SW¼ of Section 7, and is in the NE¼ of the SW¼ of Section 7.

PRACTICE EXAM 2

1.   How many acres, rounded to the nearest hundredth of an acre, are there in 230,868 ft.²?

a. 5.41 acres

b. 5.06 acres

c. 4.57 acres

d. none of the above

2.   What is the area of the triangle in the diagram below?

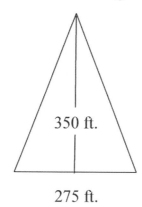

350 ft.

275 ft.

a. 48,125 ft.²

b. 96,250 ft.²

c. 43,750 ft.²

d. 51,562.1 ft.²

3.   There are 5,600 homes in Margaret's assigned area. If 4.5% of those homes sold last year, how many homes in Margaret's area sold last year?

a. 252

b. 224

c. 225

d. 220

4.   What is the interest (rounded to the nearest dollar) on a $300,000 loan for 1 year, 3 months, and 20 days at 6% interest (using the 30/360 day count convention)?

a. $23,500

b. $22,500

c. $19,000

d. $25,000

5.   Margaret is putting 15% down on a house she is purchasing for $400,000. The lender is requiring an upfront payment of 1.5% of the loan amount for private mortgage insurance. How much must Margaret deposit into escrow at the closing of this transaction?

a. $60,000

b. $65,100

c. $66,000

d. $81,200

6.   Bill's second home has an assessed value of $355,000, and no exemptions apply. The annual property tax rate is $2.25/$100). What is the annual property tax on this second home?

a. $7,875

b. $7,810

c. $7,700

d. none of the above

7.   Albert sold a house for $315,000 and received $7,875 in commission from his broker. What commission rate did Albert receive on the sale?

a. 3%

b. 3.5%

c. 2.5%

d. 2%

8.   A triangular lot with a height 135 feet and a base of 90 feet sold for $18 per square foot. What did the lot sell for?

a. $118,700

b. $109,350

c. $128,250

d. $218,700

9.   A 16,000 ft.² lot costs $22 per square foot. The 3,200 ft.² house on the lot costs $135 per square foot, and the 430 ft.² garage costs $35 per square foot. How much does this property cost?

a. $784,000

b. $799,050

c. $654,050

d. none of the above

10.   Linda's lender required a 15% down payment to obtain the mortgage on her house. The down payment amount was $64,500. What was the purchase price that Linda paid for her house?

a. $79,412

b. $129,000

c. $430,000

d. $382,500

11.   Lorraine is purchasing a house for $450,000 with 20% down and has negotiated a very favorable interest rate. However, in order to obtain this favorable interest rate, the lender requires that Lorraine pay 1.5 discount points upfront. How much will Lorraine pay the lender for these discount points?

a. $5,400

b. $6750

c. $540

d. $675

12.   A vacant lot has a fair market value of $130,000. The assessed value of the lot is 70% of its fair market value. The annual property tax mill rate is 40. What is the annual property tax on the lot?

a. $3,640

b. $5,200

c. $364

d. $520

13.   If a loan has an LTV of 85%, the property has an appraised value of $210,000, and a sales price of $215,000, what is the amount of the loan if the LTV was based on the lesser of the appraised value or the sales price?

a. $182,750

b. $210,000

c. $215,000

d. none of the above

14.   To obtain a lower interest rate for the purchase of a $300,000 condo, Joyce has arranged to pay the lender 1.5 points for a loan in the amount of 80% of the purchase price. How much will Joyce have to pay for these discount points?

a. $4,500

b. $3,000

c. $2,400

d. none of the above

15.   The outstanding balance of loans against Samantha's home is $100,000. She has just arranged to obtain a home equity line of credit of 80% of the appraised value of her home, minus the total indebtedness against her home. The amount of the line of credit is $60,000. What is the appraised value of Samantha's home?

a. $175,000

b. $225,000

c. $185,000

d. none of the above

16.   The selling price of the home Howard is purchasing is $280,000. The lender is willing to loan 80% of the lesser of the purchase price or the appraised value. If the amount the lender is willing to loan is $220,000, what is the appraised value of Howard's home?

a. $224,000

b. $275,000

c. $220,000

d. $160,000

17.   A home has a fair market value of $550,000, a homestead exemption of $100,000, an assessed value of $468,000, and a county property tax of 1.2%. What is the annual county property tax on this home?

a. $5,400

b. $5,616

c. $4,320

d. none of the above

18.   Olivia was a cooperating broker who earned 6% on the first $100,000 of a $250,000 sale. The remainder of the commission went to the listing broker, Emily. If the total commission earned on the sale was $12,750, what percentage of the remaining $150,000 did Emily receive?

a. 4%

b. 4.5%

c. 5%

d. 5.5%

19.   Kenny is a real estate salesperson who found a buyer for a home that sold for $750,000. Kenny's employing broker split the 5% commission for the sale with the listing

broker. The agreement between Kenny his employing broker provides that Kenny receive 40% of his employing broker's commission on every sale Kenny procures. What is Kenny's commission on this transaction?

a. $18,750

b. $9,375

c. $15,000

d. none of the above

20.   José paid a 5% broker's commission and $4,600 in closing costs on the sale of his condo, which had cost him $150,000 a few years earlier. If José makes a profit of $6,900 on the sale, what was the sale price of the condo?

a. $165,158 (rounded)

b. $162,737 (rounded)

c. $157,895 (rounded)

d. none of the above

21.   A residential property was purchased for $375,600. The state documentary transfer fee is $.75 for each $500 or fraction thereof. The property was purchased with $300,600 cash and an assumption of the $75,000 seller's mortgage. Assumed mortgages are exempt from the transfer fee in this state. What was the documentary transfer fee?

a. $450.75

b. $451.50

c. $450.00

d. $113.25

22.   Charles purchased a home for $350,000 with a 6% fixed-rate, fully amortized 30-year loan in the principal amount of $312,208. He makes payments of $1,872 per month. What is the amount of unpaid principal on this loan after the first month's payment?

a. $310,336

b. $310,450

c. $311,429

d. none of the above

23.   Alan and Susan's combined monthly gross income is $6,000. If a lender requires a PITI of 32%, what is the maximum PITI with which Alan and Susan can qualify?

a. $4,080

b. $1,920

c. $1,800

d. none of the above

24.   Hannah purchases a building for $3,000,000 that has a useful life of 30 years and an anticipated residual value of $750,000. After 10 years, what is the value of the building, if by "value" we mean the original cost less accumulated straight-line depreciation?

a. $2,250,000

b. $2,000,000

c. $2,150,000

d. none of the above

25.   The annual net operating income of Joel's apartment building is $210,000. An appraiser estimated the value of the property at $2,625,000. What capitalization rate did the appraiser use to arrive at her valuation?

a. 16%

b. 8%

c. 4 %

d. none of the above

26.   A small office building generates gross monthly rentals of $3,400. It also takes in $225 per month for parking fees. The fair market value of the property is $935,000. What is the monthly gross rent multiplier for this property?

a. 258 (rounded)

b. 273 (rounded)

c. $294 (rounded)

d. none of the above

27.   Tom owns a 350 yd.² rectangular lot with depth of 60 feet. What is the frontage of Tom's lot?

a. 5.83 feet

b. 17.5 feet

c. 52.5 feet

d. 6 fee

28.   George obtains a 30-year, 4½% level-payment loan of $500,000 to purchase a house. His monthly payments are $2,275. What is his interest charge for the second month?

a. $1,866.47

b. $1,873.50

c. $1,837

d. $1,875

29. A 20,000 ft.² lot costs $24 per square foot. The 3,100 ft.² house on the lot costs $130 per square foot, and the 450 ft.² garage costs $37 per square foot. How much does this property cost?

a. $591,350

b. $611,220

c. $611,323

d. $899,650

30. Charles makes payments of $1,872 per month, including 6% interest on a fixed-rate, fully amortized 30-year loan. What was the initial amount of his loan, rounded to the nearest dollar?

Monthly Payment Per $1,000 on Fixed-Rate, Fully Amortized Loans				
Rate	10-year term	15-year term	30-year term	40-year term
4%	10.125	7.397	4.775	4.180
5%	10.607	7.908	5.369	4.822
6%	11.102	8.439	5.996	5.503
7%	11.611	8.989	6.653	6.215
8%	12.133	9.557	7.338	6.954

a. $312,208

b. $281,377

c. $348,668

d. none of the above

Practice Exam 2 Answers

1.   **d.** 230,868 ft.² ÷ 43,560 ft.²/acre = 5.3 acres.

2.   **a.** The area of this triangle, as with all triangles, is equal to ½ (base × height), which in this case is ½ (275 ft. × 350 ft.) = 48,125 ft.²

3.   **a.** .045 × 5,600 = 252.

4.   **a.** The time elapsed is 360 days + 90 days +20 days = 470 days.
470 ÷ 360 = 1.305556 years. Therefore, applying our formula
Interest = Rate × Principal × Time, we get
Interest = .06/yr. × $300,000 × 1.305556 yr. = $23,500 (rounded to the nearest dollar)

5.:   **b.** In this example, Margaret must deposit into escrow enough to cover both the down payment and the upfront PMI payment. The down payment is
15% of $400,000 = $60,000. Therefore, the amount of the loan is
$400,000 - $60,000 = $340,000.
The upfront PMI payment = 1.5% of $340,000 = $5,100. Therefore, Margaret must bring to escrow $60,000 + $5,100 = $65,100.

6.   **d.** $2.25/$100 × $355,000 = $7,987.50.

7.   **c.** $7,875 ÷ $315,000 = .025, which means that Albert received a commission rate of 2.5%.

8.   **b.** The area of the triangular lot is ½ (135 ft. × 90 ft.) = 6,075 ft.². Therefore, at a cost of $18/ ft.², the lot sold for 6,075 ft.² × $18/ft.² = $109,350.

9.   **b.** Lot: 16,000 ft.² x $22/ft.² = $352,000
           House: 3,200 ft.² x 135/ft.² = $432,000
           Garage: 430 ft.² x 35/ft.² = $15,050
                        Total = $799,050

10.   **c.** 15% of the purchase price = .15 × (purchase price) = $64,500. Dividing both sides of the equation by .15, we get purchase price = $430,000.

11.   **a.** Lorraine is putting 20% of $450,000 = $90,000 down. Therefore, the loan amount is $450,000 - $90,000 = $360,000. The cost to Lorraine of the discount points would therefore be $360,000 × .015 = $5,400.

12.   **a.** Because no mention is made of property tax exemptions, we must assume that the taxable value is the assessed value, which we are told is 70% of $130,000 = $91,000. The tax rate is 40 mill = $40/$1,000; therefore, the annual property tax on the lot is
$40/$1,000 × $91,000 = $3,640.

13.   **d.** Here, LTV = .85 = (amount of the loan) ÷ $210,000. Therefore, the amount of the loan is $210,000 × .85 = $178,500.

14.   **d.** Loan amount = 80% of $300,000 = $240,000.
The cost of 1.5 points on a $240,000 loan is .015 × $240,000 = $3,600.

15. **d.** (appraised value × .8) - $100,000 = $60,000. Therefore, appraised value = $160,000 ÷ .8 = $200,000.

16. **b.** (the lesser of the appraised value or $280,000) × .8 = $220,000. (the lesser of the appraised value or $280,000) = $220,000 ÷ .8 = $275,000. Therefore, the appraised value of the home is $275,000.

17. **d.** ($468,000 - $100,000) × .012 = $4,416.

18. **b.** Olivia received 6% of $100,000 = $6,000. Therefore, Emily received $12,750 - $6,000 = $6,750. $6,750 ÷ $150,000 = .045 = 4½%.

19. **d.** Kenny's employing broker's commission is 50% of 5% of $750,000 = $18,750. Kenny's commission is 40% of $18,750 = $7,500.

20. **d.** Before the commission was paid, there was $4,600 + $150,000 + $6,900 equals $161,500 to be accounted for. Therefore, $161,500 = 95% × Sales Price. Sales Price = $161,500 ÷ .95 = $170,000.

21. **b.** $300,600 = $500 × 601.2. Therefore, because the transfer fee is $.75 for each $500 *or fraction thereof*, the transfer fee = 602 × $.75 = $451.50.

22. **d.** $312,208 × .06 ÷ 12 = $1,561.04 (first month's interest) $1,872 - $1,561.04 = $310.96 (first month's principal payment) $312,208 - $310.96 = $311,897.04 (principal balance after first month's payment).

23. **b.** Maximum PITI ÷ $6,000 = .32. Maximum PITI = $6,000 × .32 = $1,920.

24. **a.** Annual depreciation = (cost of property - residual value) ÷ useful life of property. Therefore, annual depreciation = ($3,000,000 - $750,000) ÷ 30 = $75,000. Accumulated straight-line depreciation equals $75,000 × 10 = $750,000. $3,000,000 - $750,000 = $2,250,000.

25. **b.** $210,000 ÷ $2,625,000 = 8%.

26. **d.** To calculate gross rent multipliers, we do not consider income from any source other than rents. Therefore, in this case gross monthly rent multiplier = $935,000 ÷ $3,400 = 275.

27. **c.** A square yard is 3' x 3' = 9 ft.², so the lot is 350 yd.² × 9 ft./yd.² = 3,150 ft.². Since the depth is 60 feet, the frontage is 3,150 ft. ÷ 60 feet = 52.5 feet.

28. **b.** George's per month interest rate is 4½% ÷ 12 = .375%. Therefore, the interest payment during the first month is .375% of $500,000 = $1,875. Since he paid $2,275 for the first month, $400 went to paying down the principal. Therefore, for the second month, his interest charge would be .375% of $499,600 = $1,873.50.

29.   **d.** Lot: 20,000 ft.² x $24/ft.² = $480,000
House: 3001 ft.² x $130/ft.² = $403,000
Garage: 450 ft.² x $37/ft.² = $16,650
$899,650

30.   **a.** Finding where 6% and a 30-year term intersect in the table, we obtain the number 5.996 which is the dollar amount per month per $1,000 of the initial loan.
$5.996/$1,000 = $1,872/loan amount. Therefore,
loan amount = ($1,872 ÷ $5.996) × $1,000 = $312,208 (rounded).

Monthly Payment Per $1,000 on Fixed-Rate, Fully Amortized Loans				
Rate	10-year term	15-year term	30-year term	40-year term
4%	10.125	7.397	4.775	4.180
5%	10.607	7.908	5.369	4.822
6%	11.102	8.439	5.996	5.503
7%	11.611	8.989	6.653	6.215
8%	12.133	9.557	7.338	6.954

PRACTICE EXAM 3

1.   Marvin sold his house and netted $180,000 from the sale. At the time of closing he had a mortgage with outstanding principal balance of $220,000. Closing costs were $7,000, and he paid a 5% commission on the sale. What was the selling price, rounded to the nearest dollar, of Marvin's house?

a. $407,950

b. $428,421

c. $433,989

d. $441,439

2.   A rectangular lot contains 4.7 acres and is 220 feet wide. What is the depth of the lot?

a. 1023.66 feet

b. 930.60 feet

c. 969.05 feet

d. 974.6 feet

3.   How much did David borrow at 4% if he paid $1,200 interest for a period of three months?

a. $30,000

b. $90,000

c. $48,000

d. $120,000

4.   A lender has agreed to make a loan for a condo having a purchase price and an appraised value of $140,000. The lender required PMI to cover the top 20% of the loan, which 20% turned out to be $23,800. What was the LTV of this loan?

a. 83%

b. 80%

c. 90%

d. 85%

5.   Karen takes out a loan to purchase a house with the sales price of $345,250. The amount of the mortgage note is 80% of the purchase price. If the intangible tax

in Karen's state is $1.50 for every $500 value of the note or fraction thereof, how much intangible tax would apply to this conveyance?

a. $829.50

b. $828

c. $1035.75

d. $662.40

6.   How many acres, rounded to the nearest hundredth of an acre, are there in 163,350 ft.²?

a. 3.74 acres

b. 3.84 acres

c. 3.76 acres

d. none of the above

7.   There are 3,600 homes in Angie's assigned area. If 3.5% of those homes sold last year, how many homes in Angie's area sold last year?

a. 252

b. 108

c. 126

d. 220

8.   What is the interest (rounded to the nearest dollar) on a $200,000 loan for 1 year, 4 months, and 24 days at 4.5% interest (using the 30/360 day count convention)?

a. $12,600

b. $34,233

c. $17,640

d. $25,200

9.   Karen is putting 15% down on a house she is purchasing for $240,000. The lender is requiring an upfront payment of 1.75% of the loan amount for private mortgage insurance. How much cash must Karen deposit into escrow at the closing of this transaction?

a. $36,000

b. $39,570

c. $30,600

d. $81,200

10.   Amber's second home has an assessed value of $155,000, and no exemptions apply. The annual property tax rate is $2.25/$100). What is the annual property tax on this second home?

a. $7,875

b. $7,810

c. $7,700

d. none of the above

11.   John's lender gave him an $88,000 loan based on a loan-to-value ratio (LTV) of 80% of the lesser of the appraised value of the property, which was $120,000, or the sales price. What was the sales price of John's property?

a. $110,000

b. $120,000

c. $100,000

d. none of the above

12.   Marcus has obtained a $323,000 loan to purchase a home for $380,000. What is the loan-to-value ratio of this transaction?

a. 93%

b. 80%

c. 85%

d. 84.2%

13.   Harvey's home is appraised at $250,000. The first mortgage against his home has an outstanding balance of $150,000. Harvey has just arranged to obtain a home equity line of credit in the amount of 80% of the appraised value of his home, minus the total outstanding indebtedness against the home. What is the amount of his line of credit?

a. $80,000

b. $50,000

c. $200,000

d. $120,000

14.   Margaret is purchasing a home with a purchase price of $280,000 and an appraised value of $275,000. If the lender is willing to loan 80% of the lesser of the purchase price and the appraised value, how much will be Margaret's down payment?

a. $60,000

b. $56,000

c. $55,000

d. none of the above

15.   Sally purchased a home for $195,130 with a 6% fixed-rate, fully amortized 30-year loan in the principal amount of $156,104. She makes payments of $936 per month. How much principal is retired on Sally's loan by the second month's payment?

a. $780.52

b. $156.26

c. $155.48

d. $779.74

16.   Kathy is a salesperson who receives 45% of the total commission received by her broker from the sale of a house Kathy listed. What is the broker's net share of the commission if the house sold for $845,000, the commission rate was 6%, and a cooperating broker received half of the commission?

a. $25,350

b. $13,942.50

c. $27,885.00

d. none of the above

17.   Marva is a real estate salesperson who found a buyer for a home that sold for $750,000. Marva's employing broker received a 5% commission for the sale. The agreement between the broker and Marva provides that she receive 40% of the broker's commission on every sale she procures. What is Marva's commission on this transaction?

a. $15,000

b. $18,750

c. $11,250

d. none of the above

18.   Janet sells her condo to Martha for $200,000, closing date May 16. If property taxes on the condo are $1,800 for each six-months, payable in arrears on July 1 and January 1 of each year, and if proration is calculated on the basis of a banker's year (statutory year), what is the proration amount at closing and is who credited/debited if the day of closing belongs to the buyer?

a. $450 debited to Janet

b. $1,300 debited to Janet

c. $1,350 debited to Janet

d. none of the above

19.   A residential property was purchased for $375,500. The state documentary transfer fee is $.75 for each $500 or fraction thereof. The property was purchased with $300,500 cash and an assumption of the $75,000 seller's mortgage. Assumed mortgages are exempt from the transfer fee in this state. What was the documentary transfer fee?

a. $562.50

b. $112.50

c. $450.75

d. $450.00

20.   If $7,500 is loaned for one 30-day month on the basis of simple interest, and the total amount of interest due at the end of that month is $25, what annual rate of interest was charged if interest is calculated based on a 360 day year?

a. 4%

b. 3⅓ %

c. 4⅓ %

d. none of the above

21.   Alan and Susan's monthly PITI payment is $2,450. Their lender required a PITI ratio of 32%. What is the minimum combined gross monthly income the lender required of Alan and Susan?

a. $7,656.25

b. $7,500

c. $3,602.94

d. none of the above

22.   An apartment building produces an annual gross income of $2,970,000. Vacancies and uncollectible rents are running 8%. Monthly operating expenses are $145,400. What is the annual NOI?

a. $2,587,000

b. $1,225,200

c. $1,982,400

d. none of the above

23.   The monthly net operating income of Justin's property is $35,000 and the capitalization rate is 7.5% per year. What is the value of Justin's property based on an income valuation of the property?

a. $400,000

b. $466,667 (rounded)

c. $500,000

d. none of the above

24.   Three similar properties in the area have fair market values and monthly rentals as follows: Comparable 1 — $264,600; $980. Comparable 2 — $272,640; $960. Comparable 3; $283,200; $960. What is the average monthly gross rent multiplier for these properties?

a. 283

b. 284

c. 295

d. none of the above

25.   A rectangular lot 200 feet deep and 150 feet wide has a building setback of 20 feet from each side. What is the maximum square footage of a four-story office building that can be built on this lot?

a. 104,000 ft.^{2}

b. 96,000 ft.^{2}

c. 70,400 ft.^{2}

d. 83,200 ft.^{2}

26.   Joe and Frank own a building that produces rent of $19,500 per month. Joe owns a 27% interest in the building. How much rental income from the building does Joe earn each year?

a. $63,180

b. $5,265

c. $14,235

d. $170,820

27.   Susan purchased a condo for $350,000. Three years later she sold the condo for $375,000. What percentage gross profit did she make on the sale of the condo?

a. 2.38%

b. 2.22%

c. 6.67%

d. 7.14%

28.   A rectangular lot is 325 feet wide and contains 5.8 acres. What is the depth of the lot?

a. 670.15 feet

b. 842.16 feet

c. 759.53 feet

d. 777.38 feet

29.   What is the area of the triangle in the diagram below?

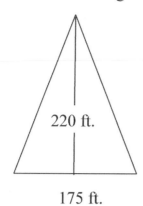

220 ft.

175 ft.

a. 19,250 ft.²

b. 77,000 ft.²

c. 43,750 ft.²

d. 38,500 ft.²

30.   A lot of land in the shape of a right triangle with height 90' ft. and base 180'sells for $45 per square foot. What is the cost of this lot?

a. $729,000

b. $243,000

c. $364,500

d. none of the above

Practice Exam 3 Answers

1. **b.** Let P stand for the selling price of the house. We know that P had to include the $180,000 that Marvin netted from the sale, the $220,000 mortgage balance, the $7,000 closing costs, and the commission, which we are told was 5% of P = .05 P. Hence,
P = $180,000 + $220,000 + $7,000 + .05 P. Subtracting .05 P from both sides of the equation and adding the amounts in the right side of the equation, we get
.95 P = $407,000. Dividing both sides of the equation by .95, we obtain
P = $428,421.

2. **b.** There are 4.7 acres × 43,560 ft.²/acre = 204,732 ft.².
204,732 ft.² ÷ 220 ft. = 930.6 ft.

3. **d.** Using the formula Interest = Rate × Principal × Time,
$1,200 = .04 × Principal × ¼ yr.
($1,200 ÷ .04) ÷ ¼ = $120,000 = Principal.

4. **d.** We are told that 20% of the loan was $23,800. Therefore,
.2 × loan amount = $23,800. Therefore,
loan amount = $23,800 ÷ .2 = $119,000.
LTV = $119,000 ÷ $140,000 = .85 = 85%.

5. **a.** The amount of the mortgage note = $345,250 × 80% = $276,200.
$276,200 ÷ $500 = 552.4. Because Karen's state imposes an intangible tax of $1.50 for every $500 value **or fraction thereof**, the transfer tax would be
553 × $1.50 = $829.50.

6. **d.** 163,350 ft.² ÷ 43,560 ft.²/acre = 3.75 acres.

7. **c.** .035 × 3,600 = 126.

8. **a.** The time elapsed is 360 days + 120 days + 24 days = 504 days.
504 ÷ 360 = 1.4 years. Therefore, applying our formula
Interest = Rate × Principal × Time, we get
Interest = .045/yr. × $200,000 × 1.4 yr. = $12,600.

9. **b.** In this example, Karen must deposit into escrow enough cash to cover both the down payment and the upfront PMI payment. The down payment is
15% of $240,000 = $36,000. Therefore, the amount of the loan is
$240,000 - $36,000 = $204,000.
The upfront PMI payment = 1.75% of $204,000 = $3,570. Therefore, Karen must bring to escrow $36,000 + $3,570 = $39,570.

10. **d.** $2.25/$100 × $155,000 = $3,487.50.

11.   **a.** $88,000 = 80\% \times$ (the lesser of $120,000 or the sales price). Therefore, $88,000 \div .8 = \$110,000 =$ (the lesser of $120,000 or the sales price), so the sales price was $110,000.

12.   **c.** $323,000 \div \$380,000 = .85 = 85\%$.

13.   **b.** ($250,000 \times .8) - \$150,000 = \$50,000$.

14.   **a.** Loan amount $= \$275,000 \times .8 = \$220,000$.
Down payment = purchase price - loan amount = $280,000 - \$220,000 = \$60,000$.

15.   **b.** $156,104 \times .06 \div 12 = \$780.52$ (first month's interest)
$936 - \$780.52 = \$155.48$ (first month's principal payment)
$156,104 - \$155.48 = \$155,948.52$ (principal balance after first month's payment).
$155,948.52 \times .06 \div 12 = \$779.74$ (second month's interest)
$936 - \$779.74 = \$156.26$ (second month's principal payment).

16.   **b.** Kathy's broker's gross is 3% of the sales price of $845,000, which is $.03 \times \$845,000 = \$25,350$. The broker's *net* is 55% of $25,350 = \$13,942.50$.

17.   **a.** The broker's commission is 5% of $750,000 = \$37,500$. Therefore, Marva's commission is 40% of $37,500 = \$15,000$.

18.   **c.** Using the banker's year of 30 days per month, at the closing Janet is in arrears in her payment of taxes by 15 days in May and $4 \times 30 = 120$ days for January through April, total 135 days. Because there are 180 days in six months of a banker's year, the per day tax rate on the $1,800 tax bill is $10. Therefore, 135 days $\times$ $10 per day $= \$1,350$, which should be debited to Janet and credited to the Martha.

19.   **c.** $300,500 = \$500 \times 601$.
$601 \times \$.75 = \$450.75$.

20.   **a.** $25 (interest) $= \$7,500 \times$ Annual Interest Rate $\div 12$.
Therefore, annual interest rate $= (\$25 \div \$7,500) \times 12 = .04 = 4\%$.

21.   **a.** $2,450 \div$ (gross monthly income) $= .32$.
Therefore, gross monthly income $= \$2,450 \div .32 = \$7,656.25$.

22.   **d.** $2,970,000 \times .08 = \$237,600$.
Annual operating expenses $= \$145,400 \times 12 = \$1,744,800$.
NOI $= \$2,970,000 - (\$237,600 + \$1,744,800) = \$987,600$.

23.   **d.** Because the *monthly* net operating income is $35,000, the annual net operating income is $35,000 \times 12 = \$420,000$. $420,000 \div 7.5\% = \$5,600,000$.

24.   **a.** Comparable 1: $264,600 \div \$980 = 270$.
Comparable 2: $272,640 \div \$960 = 284$.
Comparable 3: $283,200 \div \$960 = 295$.
$(270 + 284 + 295) \div 3 = 283$.

25. **c.** Because there is a 20 ft. setback on each side, we are left with a parcel that is 160 ft. $\times$ 110 ft. = 17,600 ft.² in area per floor. The area of 4 floors would be 4 $\times$ 17,600 ft.² = 70,400 ft.²

26. **a.** The annual rental income is \$19,500/mo. $\times$ 12 mo./yr. = \$234,000/yr. 27% of \$234,000 = \$63,180/yr.

27. **d.** Susan made \$25,000 gross profit. \$25,000 $\div$ \$300,000 = 7.14%

28. **d.** 5.8 acres x 43,560 ft.²/acre = 252,648 ft.². 252,648 ft.² $\div$ 325 = 777.38 feet.

29. **a.** The area of this triangle, as with all triangles, is equal to ½ (base $\times$ height), which in this case is ½ (220 ft. $\times$ 175 ft.) = 19,250 ft.²

30. **c.** The area of this lot is ½ (90 ft. $\times$ 180 ft.) = 8,100 ft.² Therefore, the cost of the lot is 8,100 ft.² $\times$ \$45/ft.² = \$364,500.

PRACTICE EXAM 4

1.   What is the rectangular survey system legal description of the shaded area of Section 7 in the diagram below?

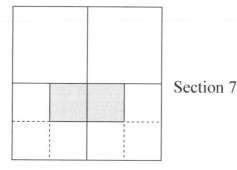 Section 7

a. SE¼ of the NE½ Section 7 and the NW¼ of the SE¼ of Section 7

b. NE¼ of the SE¼ of Section 7 and the N½ of the SW¼ of Section 7

c. NE¼ of the SE¼ of Section 7 and the SE¼ of the NE¼ of Section 7

d. NE¼ of the SW¼ of Section 7 and the NW¼ of the SE¼ of Section 7

2.   A warehouse is 20 yards wide, 25 yards long, and 30 feet high. How many cubic feet are contained in this warehouse?

a. 135,000 ft.³

b. 15,000 ft.³

c. 5,000 ft.³

d. 405,000 ft.³

3.   Kathy procured for her employing broker a listing for a condo with list price of $295,000. The seller agreed to pay the broker a commission of 5% of the sales price. Kathy's agreement with her broker is that she would receive 50% of any commission received by her broker coming from listings and sales that she procures. With the help of a cooperating broker — who had a commission split agreement with Kathy's employing broker whereby Kathy's employing broker would receive 60% and the cooperating broker would receive 40% of the commission — the house eventually sold for 95% of the list price. What was Kathy's commission on this transaction?

a. $4,203.75

b. $4,425.00

c. $3,503.13

d. $3,687.50

4.   Andrew sold his condo for $184,000 six years after he purchased it for $160,000. At what annual rate did Andrew profit from his investment?

a. 2.2% (rounded)

b. 13% (rounded)

c. 2½%

d. 15%

5.   Robert's lender is willing to loan 75% of the lesser of the purchase price of his house and the appraised value of the house. The purchase price of the house is $280,000. The loan amount is $195,000. What is the appraised value of the house?

a. $156,000

b. $260,000

c. $210,000

d. $195,000

6.   A lender requires a yield on a loan to Barbara that is .75% greater than the interest rate on the loan quoted to Barbara. How many discount points must this lender charge Barbara in order to obtain the lender's required yield if to reduce the interest rate by .15% the lender must charge one discount point?

a. 3 discount points

b. 5 discount points

c. 6 discount points

d. 4 discount points

7.   Stephen sold his house and netted $70,000 from the sale. At the time of closing he had a mortgage with outstanding principal balance of $120,000. Closing costs were $7,000, and he paid a 5% commission on the sale. What was the selling price, rounded to the nearest dollar, of Stephen's house?

a. $133,684

b. $180,500

c. $197,000

d. $207,368

8.   A lot of land in the shape of a right triangle with height 80' ft. and base 170'sells for $55 per square foot. What is the cost of this lot?

a. $748,000

b. $187,000

c. $374,000

d. none of the above

9.   A rectangular lot contains 2 acres and is 242 feet wide. What is the depth of the lot?

a. 180 feet

b. 360 feet

c. 361 feet

d. 185 feet

10.   How much did Matthew borrow at 3.2% if he paid $800 interest for a period of three months?

a. $75,000

b. $90,000

c. $100,000

d. $25,000

11.   A lender has agreed to make a loan for a condo having a purchase price and an appraised value of $162,500. The lender required PMI to cover the top 20% of the loan, which 20% turned out to be $29,250. What was the LTV of this loan?

a. 83%

b. 80%

c. 90%

d. 85%

12.   Emily takes out a loan to purchase a house with the sales price of $245,200. The amount of the mortgage note is 80% of the purchase price. If the intangible tax in Emily's state is $1.25 for every $500 value of the note or fraction thereof, how much intangible tax would apply to this conveyance?

a. $491.25

b. $307.50

c. $490

d. $662.40

13.   Evan purchased a rectangular lot measuring 125' deep by 160' along the street. Zoning regulations require a 15' setback from the street and a 10' setback along all other sides. What are the buildable dimensions of Evan's lot?

a. 115' × 145'

b. 110' × 140'

c. 100' × 140'

d. 115' × 145'

14.   Charles purchases a home with a $75,000 down payment and a loan with an LTV of 85% of the purchase price. What is the amount of the loan?

a. $425,000

b. $82,235.29

c. $500,000

d. none of the above

15. Charles is purchasing a house for $285,000. The lender requires 3.2 discount points, which amounts to $7,752. How much did Charles pay as a down payment?

a. $9,120

b. $42,750

c. $45,600

d. none of the above

16. Janet's customer, Susan, wants to buy a condo for $225,000. The best financing that Janet can find for Susan requires 18% down. How much would Susan have to come up with to handle the required down payment?

a. $45,000

b. $39,600

c. $40,500

d. none of the above

17. José purchased a home for $195,130 with a 6% fixed-rate, fully amortized 30-year loan in the principal amount of $156,104. He makes payments of $936 per month. What is the amount of interest for the second month if calculated based on a 360-day year?

a. $780.52

b. $155.48

c. $779.74

d. $156.26

18. A home has a fair market value of $550,000, a homestead exemption of $100,000, an assessed value of $468,000, a county property tax of 1.2%, and a city property tax of .75%. What is the amount of city property tax savings due to the homestead exemption?

a. $3, 510

b. $7,176

c. $2,760

d. none of the above

19. In working out a comparative market analysis for a client, all you know about the sale price of a comparable house that recently sold next door to the property your client wishes to purchase is that your competitor, Kathy, received a $1,500 commission on the sale, that Kathy received 40% of whatever her broker grossed from the sale, that the full

commission on the sale was 6%, and that Kathy's broker split the 6% commission 50-50 with the buyer's broker. How much did the comparable house sell for?

a. $62,500

b. $125,000

c. $250,000

d. none of the above

20.   Bob sold his condo to Sandra, closing date October 16. Bob had prepaid his monthly homeowner's fee of $465 on the first of the month. How much of the homeowner's fee must the buyer reimburse Bob for if a calendar year is used for the calculation and the closing day belongs to the buyer?

a. $232.50

b. $240

c. $225

d. none of the above

21.   The sales price of Logan's home was $490,000. As part of the escrow instructions, Logan agreed to pay the 6% commission and the escrow fee, which was calculated at $2.00 per thousand of purchase price plus $250. What was the amount of proceeds that Logan received from this sale?

a. $460,480

b. $459,620

c. $460,350

d. none of the above

22.   Anita purchased a home for $275,000 with a $55,000 down payment and a 5% fixed-rate loan. What is the amount of interest due for the first month?

a. $11,000

b. $10,000

c. $9,500

d. none of the above

23.   Stephen purchased a home for $200,000 with a 4 % fixed-rate, fully amortized 15-year loan in the principal amount of $172,367. He makes payments of $1,275 per month. What is the amount of unpaid principal on this loan after the first month's payment?

a. $171,258.67

b. $171,092.00

c. $171,666.56

d. none of the above

24.   What is the value of a property based on the following information?
Estimated annual gross income: $95,000
Vacancies and uncollectible rents: 7%
Annual maintenance expenses and utilities: $10,000
Annual property taxes: $9,500
Annual insurances: $1,500
Monthly mortgage payment: $2,500
Capitalization rate: 9.5%

a. $393,159 (rounded)

b. $708,947 (rounded)

c. $778,947 (rounded)

d. none of the above

25.   If the annual net operating income of a property is $74,000 and the capitalization rate is 7.5% per year, what would be the value of the property based on an income valuation of the property?

a. $986,667 (rounded)

b. $933,334 (rounded)

c. $98,667 (rounded)

d. none of the above

26.   Homes comparable to Natalie's in the area have an average monthly gross rent multiplier of 280. The fair market value of Natalie's home is $1,743,000. Using the gross rent multiplier approach, what monthly rent should Natalie get for renting her home?

a. $6,225

b. $8,715

c. $6,214 (rounded)

d. none of the above

27.   Joanne is a broker who obtained a 6% listing agreement to sell a house. She sold the house and obtained a commission of $29,130. For how much did the house sell?

a. $485,500

b. $971,000

c. $405,500

d. none of the above

28.   A building depreciates by 3% each year. How many years will it take for the building to be worth only 40% of its initial value?

a. 30 years

b. 20 years

c. 10 years

d. 13⅓ years

29.   Karen financed the purchase of her condo with an 80% loan at a fixed annual rate of 4½%. Karen paid $1,425 interest the first month. How much did Karen pay for the condo?

a. $380,000.00

b. $475,000.00

c. $316,666.67

d. $395,833.33

30.   Tom, a salesperson, sold a ½ acre lot for $21 per square foot. The commission rate Tom's broker received was 7%, and Tom split the commission with his broker 50-50. How much did Tom earn on the sale?

a. $32,016.60

b. $16,008.30

c. $15,246

d. none of the above

Practice Exam 4 Answers

1. **d.** Because the shaded area extends into two distinct quarters of the section, we need to analyze each of the separate shaded areas separately. The area on the left is in the SW¼ of Section 7, and is in the NE¼ of the SW¼ of Section 7. The area on the right is in the SE¼ of Section 7, and is in the NW¼ of the SE¼ of Section 7.

2. **a.** The first thing we must do to perform calculations on problems that contain mixed units of measure — as does this example — is to convert all measurements to the same dimension. Because the question asks for how many cubic feet, it makes sense to convert yards into feet, rather than feet into yards. Doing this, the volume of this warehouse is (20 yd. × 3 ft./yd.) × (25 yd. × 3 ft./yd.) × 30 ft. = 135,000 ft.³

3. **a.** The house sold for 95% of $295,000 = .95 × $295,000 = $280,250. Therefore, the commission paid by the seller = 5% of $280,250 = 0.05 × $280,250 = $14,012.50. Kathy's employing broker received 60% of this commission = 0.6 × $14,012.50 = $8,407.50. Kathy received 50% of the commission received by her broker, which is 0.5 × $8,407.50 = $4,203.75.

4. **c.** Andrew's profit on his condo was $184,000 - $160,000 = $24,000. Because this $24,000 profit was spread over six years, Andrew's annual profit was $24,000 ÷ 6 = $4,000. Therefore, the annual rate of profit was $4,000 ÷ $160,000 = .025 = 2½%.

5. **b.** Because 75% of the purchase price ($280,000) = $210,000, but the loan amount was only $195,000, we know that the appraised value of the house was less than the purchase price. In fact, we know that 75% of the appraised value of the house = $195,000. Therefore, the appraised value of the house = $195,000 ÷ .75 = $260,000.

6. **b.** Since charging one discount point will raise the effective yield by .15%, the number of discount points needed are .75% ÷ .15% = 5 discount points.

7. **d.** Let P stand for the selling price of the house. We know that P had to include the $70,000 that Stephen netted from the sale, the $120,000 mortgage balance, the $7,000 closing costs, and the commission, which we are told was 5% of P = .05 P. Hence, P = $70,000 + $120,000 + $7,000 + .05 P. Subtracting .05 P from both sides of the equation and adding the amounts in the right side of the equation, we get .95 P = $197,000. Dividing both sides of the equation by .95, we obtain P = $207,368 (rounded).

8. **c.** The area of this triangular lot is ½ (80 ft. × 170 ft.) = 6,800 ft.² Therefore, the cost of the lot is 6,800 ft.² × $55/ft.² = $374,000.

9. **b.** 2 acres = 2 × 43,560 ft.² = 87,120 ft.². 87,120 ft.² ÷ 242 ft. = 360 ft.

10. **c.** Using the formula Interest = Rate × Principal × Time,
$800 = .032 × Principal × ¼ yr.
($800 ÷ .032) ÷ ¼ = $100,000 = Principal.

11. **c.** We are told that 20% of the loan was $29,250. Therefore,
.2 × loan amount = $29,250. Therefore,
loan amount = $29,250 ÷ .2 = $146,250.
LTV = $146,250 ÷ $162,500 = .90 = 90%.

12. **a.** The amount of the mortgage note = $245,200 × 80% = $196,160.
$276,200 ÷ $500 = 392.32. Because Emily's state imposes an intangible tax of $1.25 for
every $500 value **or fraction thereof**, the transfer tax would be
393 × $1.25 = $491.25.

13. **c.** The zoning regulations require that the depth of the lot (125') be reduced by 15 ' +
10' = 25' and that the length of the lot (160') be reduced by 10' + 10' = 20'. Therefore, the
dimensions of the buildable area of the lot are 100' × 140'.

14. **c.** $75,000 is 15% of the purchase price, so the purchase price is
$75,000 ÷ .15 = $500,000.

15. **b.** The loan amount is $285,000 - (the down payment).
$7,752 = .032 × ($285,000 - (the down payment)) = $9,120 - (.032 × (the down payment)).
$1,368 = .032 × (the down payment)
the down payment = $1,368 ÷ .032 = $42,750.

16. **c.** $225,000 × .18 = $40,500.

17. **c.** $156,104 × .06 ÷ 12 = $780.52 (first month's interest)
$936 - $780.52 = $155.48 (first month's principal payment)
$156,104 - $155.48 = $155,948.52 (principal balance after first month's payment).
$155,948.52 × .06 ÷ 12 = $779.74 (second month's interest).

18. **d.** $100,000 × .0075 = $750.

19. **b.** Kathy's commission is 40% of her broker's gross. Therefore, her broker's gross is
$1,500 ÷ .40 = $3,750. This means that 3% of the sales price = $3,750.
Therefore, sales price = $3,750 ÷ .03 = $125,000.

20. **b.** The number of days the buyer must reimburse Bob for is 31-15 = 16. The daily
rate of the homeowner's fee for October was $465 ÷ 31 = $15. Therefore the buyer must
reimburse Bob in an amount of $15 × 16 = $240.

21. **d.** Commission paid = $490,000 × .06 = $29,400.
Escrow fee = ($2.00 × 490) + $250 = $1,230.
Net proceeds of sale = $490,000 - ($29,400 + $1,230) = $459,370.

22. **d.** Loan amount = $275,000 - $55,000 = $220,000.
First month interest = ($220,000 × .05) ÷ 12 = $916.67.

23.   **c.** $\$172,367 \times .04 \div 12 = \$574.56$ (first month's interest)

$\$1,275 - \$574.56 = \$700.44$ (first month's principal payment)

$\$172,367 - \$700.44 = \$171,666.56$ (principal balance after first month's payment).

24.   **b.** $\$95,000 \times .07 = \$6,650$ (vacancy and uncollectible rents losses).

$\$95,000 - \$6,650 = \$88,350$ (effective gross income).

$\$88,350 - \$21,000$ (operating expenses) $= \$67,350$ (NOI). *Note that monthly mortgage payments are disregarded when calculating net operating income.*

$\$67,350 \div .095 = \$708,947$ (rounded).

25.   **a.** $\$74,000 \div 7.5\% = \$986,667$ (rounded).

26.   **a.** $\$1,743,000 \div 280 = \$6,225$.

27.   **a.** $\$29,130 \div .06 = \$485,500$.

28.   **b.** To be worth 40% of its initial value, the building would have to depreciate by 60%. Since the building depreciates at 3%/yr., it takes $60\% \div 3\%$/yr. $= 20$ years.

29.   **b.** $(\$1,425 \times 12) \div 4.5\% = \$380,000$, which represents 80% of the cost of the condo. Therefore, the cost of the condo is $\$380,000 \div 80\%$ equals $\$475,000$.

30.   **b.** ½ acre is 43,560 ft.² $\div 2 = 21,780$ ft.². 21,780 ft.² x $\$21$/ft.² $= \$457,380$. Tom's commission was 3.5% of $\$457,380 = \$16,008.30$

INDEX

Made in the USA
Lexington, KY
21 September 2015